Humanity for Prisoners

Doug Tjapkes

HFP Humanity
for Prisoners
Action with Compassion

All writing is a form of prayer

—John Keats

Humanity for Prisoners?

Published and Printed by DPZ Technology, LLC
Grand Rapids, MI
United States of America
All rights reserved

ISBN: 978-1-939909-47-3

This book is available at:

www.dpztechnology.com

"Doug, Thank you for your precious care for Prisoners"

—Sister Helen Prejean

Foreword

I think my love for prisoners started in high school when I studied corrections in social studies. The idea of rehabilitation, owning up to our mistakes and transforming our lives, with support, made sense to me. When I was a first-year law student I was hired as the student director of my law school's inmate assistance program. I interviewed prisoners and answered their legal questions. I connected with these men and women in unexpected ways. My passion for working with prisoners grew. Through the last 30 years of law practice and teaching, my passion for working with prisoners continues to grow. I have learned that it is important to: Listen when no one else would. Be the only visitor. Teach my students that the practice of law is a helping profession. Help unpopular clients and causes. Learn not to judge. Be compassionate.

Not all of us are cut out to work with prisoners. But Doug Tjapkes is, and he has dedicated the last 20+ years to doing just that. Doug is a staunch advocate for adequate medical and mental health care, fair and humane living conditions, respect, and compassion. Doug meets each prisoner where he is, assists when he can and is straightforward when he can't. Humanity for Prisoners (HFP) is dedicated to helping Michigan prisoners through "action with compassion." This book furthers Doug's mission by sharing with us a collection of 100 of his best blogs advocating for criminal justice and prison reform. These straightforward and honest stories teach us about the true meaning of rehabilitation and how our prisons continue to fall short. But they are also stories of commitment. Stories of hope. Stories striving to bring people together.

On December 21, 2008, Doug wrote: "There are atheists, agnostics, evangelicals, protestants, Catholics, Jews, liberals, conservatives...you name it. But there is a two-strand cord that binds us all together: We agree that all prisoners deserve humane treatment, and we believe that wrongful convictions are not acceptable."

Don't we all deserve humane treatment? Don't we all agree that sending the wrong person to prison is not acceptable? As citizens, we are responsible for our criminal justice system and our prisons. I hope these stories will inspire you to "take action with compassion," to do your part to make our criminal justice system fair for all, and truly rehabilitative.

Marla Mitchell-Cichon, Professor of Law and Director
Western Michigan University Cooley Law School Innocence Project
2016 Champion of Justice: State Bar of Michigan

Table of Contents

We don't need Doug, we need you!

Sunday, August 12, 2018

Keep up the good work, Doug. We need people like you!

As a young broadcast journalist, my radio editorials used to bring in a lot of comments like that. But that's about as far is it went.

In the City of Holland, for example, back in the days before Michigan's Open Meetings Act, I badgered the city council mercilessly for holding regular secret meetings. The people loved it, but nobody ever did anything about it.

Fast forward to today.

I'm not writing radio editorials anymore, but the pieces that I post on this blog site are just as direct. But I'm going to tell you something. If mass incarceration is going to get serious attention, if sinfully lengthy sentences are going to get reduced, if prison overcrowding is going to be dealt with, if the number of wrongful convictions is going to be reduced, if prison conditions are going to be improved, if spiritual communities are going to change their attitudes about those behind bars, it's not going to happen because of something I wrote. It's because somebody who reads what I write decides that enough is enough!

No, we don't need another Doug Tjapkes. Society is stuck with him for now.

We need you!

We need people who will go to the polls and vote out of office those politicians who want to be tough on crime by imposing long sentences and building more prisons.

We need people who don't just nod their heads when they read our blogs, but who, instead, email or call their state legislators regarding prison reform, prison conditions and mass incarceration.

We need people, regardless of age, who will get off their butts and work in soup kitchens, carry picket signs for refugees, crusade for better senior citizen care, and assist with prisoner re-entry.

We need people who will insist to their church fathers that the only mission fields aren't overseas, that teaching Bible lessons isn't the only way to help prisoners, and that if ex-offenders aren't appreciated in their pews, the EVERYONE WELCOME sign should be taken down.

I conclude with this quote from a church newsletter:

The opposite of love is not hate, it's indifference....
The opposite of life is not death, it's complacency.

Healthcare delayed is healthcare denied!
Monday, July 30, 2018

We're seeing a disturbing trend in Michigan prison healthcare, and I find it upsetting. It can be described in one word: delay.

John has a cyst in his throat, near the vocal cords, and health care says he needs surgery. Yet it doesn't happen.

New tests show that Scott's cancer has metastasized and is spreading along his spine and his neck. He needs to see his oncologist now. Yet it doesn't happen.

David is in terrible pain. They say he needs thoracic surgery. Yet it doesn't happen.

We are blessed to have a team of wonderful physicians on our panel of consultants, and they are constantly frustrated and alarmed by these delays. It's as if the prison healthcare people are thinking along the same lines as Mark Twain: "Never put off till tomorrow what may be done day after tomorrow just as well."

One has to wonder whether it is a simple issue of procrastination, by unconcerned and uncaring people who are just collecting their paychecks. Or is it something deeper than that? Sometimes we see clear evidence that some individuals in the corrections system believe that prisoners deserve nothing, and that, in fact, there is nothing wrong with additional punishment beyond that of incarceration. What other explanations can there be for postponing or even denying needed treatment, surgery or x-ray? For refusing to honor or allow post-op procedures? For denying pain meds when there is proven legitimacy?

Believing that all behind bars are created in the image of God, our HFP mission statement deals with that very topic, saying that we do what we do "**in order to alleviate suffering beyond the just administration of their sentences**."

As proof that the Michigan Department of Corrections has a problem in this area, I must point out that we remain busy responding to complaints like those listed above. Approximately 15% of all calls to our office have something to do with medical and/or healthcare issues. We've logged about 60 this month!

I wonder if the professionals who work for Corizon, the healthcare provider for Michigan prisons, have read their own company's statement: **As the correctional healthcare pioneer and leader for 40 years, Corizon Health provides client partners with high quality healthcare and reentry services that will improve the health and safety of our patients, reduce recidivism and better the communities where we live and work.**

Yeah, right!

No concern, no compassion, no problem
Saturday, August 25, 2018

The year was 1976.

As a semi-truck passed through Grand Haven on US 31, a distraught woman jumped from the tractor, and ran down the street screaming that she had been raped. City police stopped the truck a few blocks later and took the driver into custody.

It took days to sort out the story, but the Grand Haven Tribune chose to publish the name of the man right away, even though he had not been charged.

As the newsman for my radio station, holding up on the man's ID, I pressed then-Prosecutor Wes Nykamp about charges against that driver. He cautioned me to wait...there was more to the story. And indeed there was! The woman was arrested and charged with filing a false report. The driver was released.

But the damage was done. The man's name should not have appeared in our newspaper, and *my critical editorial on the topic captured first prize in the State Bar of Michigan Advancement of Justice competition.* That prestigious award remains here in my office.

Fast forward to 2018. A mentally ill old white man is accused of urinating on a little black girl and uttering racial slurs. Channel 8 immediately releases his name. The NAACP demands that the poor old sucker be charged with a hate crime. His picture is shown on newscast after newscast.

The Kent County Prosecutor, however, did not rush to charge the man. Instead, once again, turns out there was more to the story. The naughty little kids made up the story. The old man was released.

But the damage was done, and nobody even bothers to apologize.

Back in the 70s, it was a poor, hard-working black man from Alabama, with a wife and kids, whose name got smeared. This month, it was an elderly white man struggling with mental issues whose name got unnecessarily smeared.

The rush to get a scoop topped being fair or even, Lord help us, compassionate.

I bring all of this to your attention not to boast about a good decision that I made, but to stress, once again, the importance of showing fairness and kindness to the "little guy," the one less fortunate, the one who probably cannot speak for himself.

That's exactly why we're in this prisoner advocacy business. Inmates feel this type of rejection and unconcern regularly. For them, it's part of life.

A framed verse from Proverbs is on our office wall: **Speak up for those who cannot speak for themselves.**

I've said it before. It's "Jesus work."

Christians, some hot, some cold
Thursday, September 20, 2018

I *love* the people we work with! I mean it!

Some have been wrongly convicted. *I hurt for them.* Some of been wronged by our so-called justice system. *I'm angry with them.* Many know they've screwed up, and are genuinely sorry. *I sense their longing for forgiveness.* Regardless of the attitudes of these men and women behind bars, one thing is certain: The façade is gone. They know why they're there, they're resigned to it, and there's not a darn thing they can do about it.

In these circumstances, many, predictably, are shunned. Only 12% of them even get a prison visit! The more years behind bars, the more family members and friends start flaking off.

And so, when Michigan prisoners discover that someone cares, our love and compassion are unconditional, and we'll do our level best to help in any way that we can, the response is amazing! It's exactly what can be expected when a straggly team of caring people try to model an itinerant preacher who stated, in these exact words, "I was in prison and you visited me."

Needing the dollars to carry out this work, we make a strong appeal to the Christian community. Over the years some churches and many devoted individuals have faithfully responded. I know better, and yet, I'm deeply saddened when some responses don't match my zeal and enthusiasm.

An evangelical church: ***We have decided to support only those missions where Jesus is taught.***

A former donor: ***We prefer to support programs where Bibles are handed out and Christian principles are discussed.***

7

And most recently this message from one of the area's thriving mega churches: ***...this is not something we are willing to invest our time and resources in.*** This is the same church that boldly states in its literature: Everything we do is about lifting high the name of Jesus Christ.

I like the words of gay theologian Dr. Rembert Truluck when discussing Jesus getting baptized by John the Baptist:

...what the baptism of Jesus really means is in the fact that Jesus identified with the people, not with the prophet or with the ritual. <u>Jesus joined with and identified with the multitudes of people from every walk of life who were strangers, sick people, unclean people, rejected and outcast people, feeble and confused people, and with the people who were hurting and wounded by the false abusive religion</u> that John came to challenge.

HFP: down in the trenches, touching hundreds of lives like these, and loving it!

One more on the subject, then we'll move on
Monday, September 24, 2018

I promise to let this go, because forgiveness and kindness are also key ingredients in the Christian walk. But honestly, I have a real problem when one of our area's most popular and well-attended churches says, about (our) prison ministry, "...this is not something we are willing to invest our time and resources in."

That reply came to a simple inquiry whether we might be able to tell church leaders the story about HFP's work with Michigan prisoners.

What if we had given that response to the people who came to us when they didn't know where to turn?

To those caring prisoners who begged us to find a place for Old Bill so that he could be paroled and die in freedom.

To the guy with sleep apnea who wasn't allowed to have his CPap breathing device.

To those caring prisoners who begged us to intervene at Carol's Public Hearing so she could spend her final weeks on earth at home with family.

To the prisoners' mom who wasn't allowed to see her sons because of unpaid traffic tickets.

To the mentally ill women being abused in the critical unit.

To a wife when the prison wouldn't provide the location of her dying husband.

To the elderly inmate who found his long-lost son.

To the guy with bad eyes who finally got a pair of reading glasses.

Sorry Mary. Sorry Nathan. Sorry Willie. Sorry Johnny. Sorry Patricia. *This is not something we are willing to invest our time and resources in?*

It's not up to me to advise any church to dig into roots of Christianity, but I'd like to quote one of the early church fathers here. **Saint Augustine of Hippo** was an early Christian theologian whose writings influenced the development of Western Christianity. He was viewed as one of the most important church fathers in Western Christianity.

Among his many profound quotes is this one:

"What does love look like? It has the hands to help others. It has the feet to hasten to the poor and needy. It has eyes to see misery and want. It has the ears to hear the sighs and sorrows of men. That is what love looks like."

And that, it seems to me, is exactly what a church might want to "invest its time and resources in."

We can say for a certainty that it's the rule of thumb here at HFP.

4th of July: Mixed Emotions
Tuesday, July 3, 2018

Government of the people, by the people, for the people, shall not perish from the earth.

—Abraham Lincoln

I'm convinced Ol' Honest Abe was right, but I'll bet he'd have some second thoughts if he saw what was going on today: People in high office flirting with autocracy, serious threats to freedom of speech, dangerous talk against a free press, making a mockery of the Statue of Liberty's words of welcome.

But on this Fourth of July, I'm still going to celebrate.

"To every thing there is a season," says the teacher in Ecclesiastes: "**...A time to weep**, and **a time to laugh...**"

That's especially true on our country's birthday. I'm thinking we should do both.

On this Independence Day, let's once again take a moment to celebrate and give thanks for the document that bears these words:

We hold these truths to be self-evident, that all men are created equal, that they are endowed by their Creator with certain unalienable rights, that among these are life, liberty and the pursuit of happiness.

But, July 4 is also a somber time for the U.S. of A. Sometimes I get concerned that our political unrest, our Supreme Court vacancy and our shameful mishandling of migrant families seem to get all the attention. Meanwhile, it feels like we're just getting hardened and calloused about our terrible incarceration numbers...the worst in the world!

11

The UCLA says the "land of the free" is the world's leading jailer. And it's true! While the United States boasts about 5% of the world's population, the number behind bars jumps to 25%! Largely because of our "tough on crime" policies of the 80s and 90s, we have well over 2 million people in cages. It breaks down in rounded figures this way: 1.2 million in state prisons, 750,000 in local jails, and 217,000 in federal facilities.

I'm not saying you shouldn't have fun with family and friends on this holiday. I'm going to. I'm just saying that a lot of others wish they could do the same, and it won't be happening.

Keep this in mind: While Americans spend over $7 billion on food for 4th of July cookouts and picnics, our nation continues to spend over $80 billion on incarceration each year! To bring it closer to home, Michigan spends $36,000 a year to keep one person behind bars. Pure Michigan keeps people in prison longer than most states. Pure Michigan's rate of incarceration is far higher per crime and per capita than any of the other Great Lakes states.

Says Mark Twain: **Patriotism is supporting your country all the time, and your government when it deserves it.**

On this Independence Day, while seeing the importance of taking a stand as well as the disastrous effects of complacency, let's not only give thanks for our country. Let's vow to be involved.

HAPPY BIRTHDAY, USA! God shed his grace on thee.

Prisoner medical co-pay: A terrible idea!
Tuesday, June 5, 2018

If your doctor charged a $500 co-pay for every visit, how bad would your health have to get before you made an appointment?

That's the question Wendy Sawyer asked last year, in a Prison Policy Initiative blog. She was talking about the shameful co-pay policy for prisoners. 42 states have co-pay policies, ranging from $3.50 to $8 per visit. Here in the State of Michigan, prisoners are charged $5 for every visit to the health center. BUT, keep in mind the prisoner pay scale. Michigan inmates can earn as little as 75 cents a day, or at the peak, up to about $3.35 per day. So, according to the estimates calculated by PPI, the average Michigan prisoner would have to work 35 hours a week to make one co-payment. That's just unacceptable!

I bring all of this up because I just learned that Illinois lawmakers have eliminated the medical co-pay plan for prisoners. Illinois prisoners make 5 cents an hour, so the $5 co-pay was roughly equivalent to a month's wages.

The main argument for medical co-pay for prisoners is to discourage frivolous visits. Now, just as in the free world, I'm sure you might find a few hypochondriacs behind bars. But really, how many people do you know who just love to go to the doctor, and who cannot wait for the next visit? And if we're talking expense, these tiny co-payments certainly cannot make much of a dent in the cost of medical care for prisoners.

In an office where we respond to 20 messages from prisoners per day, 7 days a week, you can bet that we hear complaints about medical co-pay. Especially when a prisoner finally breaks down and agrees to give up a week's wages, and the PA tells him to take two aspirins and get out of there! Sometimes they charge for doing absolutely nothing. Not even any medical advice!

13

Our congratulations to the State of Illinois. It's way past time for Michigan lawmakers to consider the same action.

Back to Wendy Sawyer again:

Out-of-reach co-pays in prisons and jails have two unintended but inevitable consequences which make them counterproductive and even dangerous. First, when sick people avoid the doctor, disease is more likely to spread to others in the facility – and into the community, when people are released before being treated. Second, illnesses are likely to worsen as long as people avoid the doctor, which means more aggressive (and expensive) treatment when they can no longer go without it. Correctional agencies may be willing to take that risk and hope that by the time people seek care, their treatment will be someone else's problem. But medical co-pays encourage a dangerous waiting game for incarcerated people, correctional agencies, and the public – which none of us can afford.

Amen and Amen!

Another sad tale of life's final hours behind bars
Wednesday, May 30, 2018

This is the story of a prisoner who experienced a taste of hell on earth. And it didn't have to happen that way.

We never got to meet Terry.

The first we heard about her, and her plight, was late last year. The mother of her special friend contacted us, saying the 69-year-old woman was suffering from cancer. She had had at least two surgical procedures. The reason for the call to HFP was the shameful treatment Terry was receiving. *A corrections officer was not only abusive and demeaning, but had also refused to undo her shackles and allow her to go to the bathroom.*

We heard nothing further until a few days ago.

"Terry is in a lot of pain because they ran out of morphine. The family can't find out anything."

Then her brother reached out to us.

I believe she is gravely ill, maybe terminal (not sure). As I am Terry's Patient Advocate, I'm wondering why no one from the prison is keeping in touch with me regarding her condition. Do you know what the prison's responsibility is in regard to prisoners in her condition?

The next day.

An officer let an inmate see Terry today. Terry is in a lot of pain and wants to die. Don't know the exact facts but heard they ran out of morphine to alleviate her pain. How inhumane. The inmate who saw Terry called Terry's brother with this extremely disturbing news.

The next day.

As we were talking to our daughter tonight someone came to tell her that Terry had passed away. Another inmate did get to see her today thanks to some compassionate officers and she had a morphine drip and was a little more comfortable but still wanted to die. So I'm thinking that none of her family got to visit her. That is so sad. It's so comforting to know that HFP is there ready to jump on this case. Thank you ever so much for caring.

It grieves me to report that we did nothing. Breathed a prayer for her. That was it. We were tripping over ourselves trying to get better care, but sadly, it was too little too late.

Thank God there's no more cruelty, no more pain, no more suffering for Terry.

There'll be another unfortunate prisoner in line for similar experiences tomorrow. We'll be here. We'll try harder.

Cold temp/Hot topic
Friday, May 11, 2018

Maurice Carter was freezing!

I was granted special permission to visit him in his hospital room at the Duane L. Waters medical facility, a part of the Michigan prison system. He was in the final stages of Hepatitis C, and eventually would have his sentence commuted for medical reasons. But right now, he was fully clothed in a hospital bed, locked up in tiny, grey room.

"Can't you get another blanket, Maurice?"

"Well, I asked for one."

An unconcerned corrections officer, assigned to guard Maurice so he wouldn't try to escape, paid no attention. I don't know if Maurice ever got his blanket. That was back in 2004.

I'd forgotten about that incident until I chatted with a guy who recently had visited a Michigan prison psych unit while on special assignment. He explained that it was exceptionally cold in there. As he left the facility, he tried making conversation with an officer who was bundled up in his own coat. My friend kidded him about staying warm. The guard saw no reason for discussion, and had a curt response. "These guys are prisoners," he said. "You think we're going to do anything to make them comfortable?"

Under different circumstances, I could hear Jesus saying, **"I was cold in prison and you gave me a blanket,"** or, **"you turned up the heat."**

This summer, it'll be a different story. There'll be reports during the warm weather months of extreme heat in prisons, also resulting in serious discomfort.

The issue isn't hot or cold temps. It's defining what we hope to accomplish. Are we here to punish, or are we here to rehabilitate?

I'm reading impressive numbers about a reduction of the recidivism rate here in Michigan, due to some positive program improvements. Director Heidi Washington and her administration are to be commended for this.

But attitude trickle-down is equally important. If Director Washington's goal is rehabilitation, the wardens whom she appoints will also reflect that attitude. And with common-sense wardens in place, officers under them will soon get a clear picture as to the attitude and atmosphere that are expected. It's not going to happen overnight. But if we can improve the recidivism rate, we can also improve the departmental attitude. And that could and should improve the comfort rate.

Encouraging, or even simply allowing, discomfort because "these are just prisoners" is not acceptable.

I tell you the truth. Whatever you did for the least of these brothers (and sisters) of mine, you did for me.

Cold temperatures, cold attitudes, cold comments...they all hit my hot button.

Are we angry about this week's news stories? We should be!

Thursday, March 29, 2018

It's always someone else who gets wrongly convicted, right? Wrong!

Just this week in the news came the Nevest Coleman story from Chicago. DNA testing proved that the White Sox groundskeeper was innocent. He served 23 years for a crime someone else had committed. Then today came a second story, this in Michigan: Richard Phillips was released. Innocent. He had served 45 years!

No one says "Oops." No one says, "Sorry." And both of these kind men smile, express gratitude for their release, and try to jump-start their lives.

I'm sorry, but I think they should be mad as hell!

And so should we!

It was Maurice Carter's wrongful conviction that sucked me into this business.

19

Since that time my life has been touched by *so many* wrongly-convicted people. Today I started jotting down names...all are white, and most of them mid-to-upper income. Take a look,

An industrialist.
A business owner.
A financial adviser.
A housewife.
An employed laborer.
An account executive.
An independent contractor.
A teacher.
A doctor.
A general manager.

This list of fine, hard-working citizens proves that it can happen to anyone. Even you. Even me. And don't just assume that high priced lawyers can get you off. Extensive efforts and appeals by legal experts, family and friends, were not enough to help these people. Injustice conquered.

I cannot stress enough how easy it is to get into prison, and how difficult it is to get out.

It can be as simple as a family feud, a misunderstanding, a terrible accident, a troubled relationship, a struggle with depression or some other sort of mental illness—the kind of things that we all have faced or likely will face in a lifetime.

Mix in factors such as "tunnel vision" by police investigators, and win/loss records of prosecutors who are elected to office, and you have a recipe that can change a life forever. It has happened over and over again in the past. It's happening now. It'll happen again.

My reason for posting still another wrongful conviction blog is to remind that the system is not always correct, not always fair, not always just. Cops, prosecutors, and judges, while serving us well in most cases, are not infallible. Some (gasp) are criminals themselves.

Good Christians; good citizens—regardless of belief—*must* take an interest. Some of my friends contend that 10-15% of our prisoners are innocent. And that doesn't include those who have been over-charged or over sentenced. State officials reluctantly concede that the figure is more realistically around 3%. **Over 1,000 people in our Michigan Prison system who are innocent?** That's a curse! That's a blight!

Shameful, shameful, shameful!

Not acceptable.

Neither is sitting in our easy chair, clucking our teeth.

That church sign saying ALL ARE WELCOME—is it true?
Thursday, March 22, 2018

"Over and over again, when people exit the prison system, they say to the churches who visited them behind bars, 'I'm out. I'm here!' And those churches then explain that prison ministry is something they do 'in there,' and 'we don't really want ex-offenders in our building.'"

The words of Fr. Jared Cramer in our HUMANITY FOR PRISONERS video.

It's a sad reality.

I guess we might expect the world to reject ex-offenders. "Go ahead and release them, but I don't want them in my neighborhood." But, it must hurt Jesus, who loved to quote from the Old Testament about his reason for being here (**He has sent me here to proclaim freedom for the prisoners and recovery of sight for the blind, to release the oppressed...**) to see his church shy away from that very element of society.

Many years ago when we lost our first office space in downtown Muskegon, I met with the trustees of a well-known inner city church thinking they might give me a little closet space in which to do our business. I was nearly shamed out of the meeting by a board member who was convinced I wanted to put dangerous criminals back on the street

In another situation, as our needs for expanded office space became urgent, I met with a church that had room to spare. We were quickly shunned because the church has a children's day care center on the same campus. Unsavory people might be entering our doors.

In a similar discussion with still another church, it was explained that a deciding factor would be whether "clients of the ministry—former inmates—would be meeting in our offices on a regular basis?"

Sad to say, our answer would have to be, "Yes." We have an ex-offender volunteer who works in our office weekly. We're hoping to hire another ex-offender, upon his release, as a full-time employee. We love to have former prisoners speak on our behalf in public meetings. We consider them family.

I'm not pointing fingers. Heck, I'm a part of that body. Maybe if the church were aware of all of the skeletons in my closet, and the demons that still chase me after four-score years, I might not be welcome either.

But, thank God, the message of Easter is that **ALL** are welcome!

Dr. Luke quoted Jesus as saying, "It is not the healthy who need a doctor, but the sick..."

In this season of Lent, it's the perfect time to soften our thoughts about those bearing a stigma, and who are perceived to be "different."

We're all in this together.

Marching for a cause. A great idea!
Thursday, February 22, 2018

There's a Chinese proverb, says Father Greg Boyle, that says, ***The beginning of wisdom is to call things by the right name.***

I'm thinking about Fr. Boyle's explanation this morning, as I'm reading and hearing accounts of kids responding to the school massacre in Florida. In his book, BARKING TO THE CHOIR, Fr. Boyle says, "*We want to find the right name for what was done to us, for what turned us around, for what is happening to us now. We all want to find our maximum capacity. And when that desire is strong enough, we find the legs to walk us through the hallway, down the path, on the Good Journey.*"

He was referring, or course, to former gang members. But the words also seem to apply to the thousands and thousands of demonstrators who are grabbing headlines today.

God bless these kids, who—unlike many state and federal legislators—**have found the right name** for what was done to them. They're now "finding the legs" to keep walking on what is certainly a good journey!

I love to see people marching for good.

I love to see old film clips of the civil rights marches! I loved it when women marched on Washington! I love to see teenagers holding public office holders accountable for their shameful inaction...marching to their state houses, marching to the nation's capital, marching to the white house.

My hope, my prayer, is that someday we'll see this kind of support right here in Michigan, when it comes to issues involving prisoners. Like the topic of guns, prisons and prisoners are not popular, either.

I'm hearing about wrongly convicted persons who served years of prison time for a crime they did not commit, yet cannot collect the money the state promised them.

I'm hearing about prisoners deserving clemency for a variety of very justifiable reasons, yet so far, no hint of a heart by this Governor.

I'm hearing rumbles about parole reform that would include "presumptive parole," meaning that deserving inmates would get out at their earliest release date. Yet, no action.

May the determination and optimism of these courageous teenagers be contagious!

May God give us the wisdom and the insight to "call things by the right name." And then to find our legs to walk the good journey!

Unlike the kids, I'm 81, and in, what we politely call, the "sunset years." But in my mind I'm marching!

Critical issues affecting prisoners, like those touching teenagers, deserve our attention. Now.

They're not numbers; they're people!
Sunday, February 18, 2018

My friend Troy argues that, according to the State of Michigan, he's not a person.

As he researched Freedom of Information Act requests, he learned that "persons" could be entitled to such information. Said the state: ***'Person' means an individual, corporation, limited liability company, partnership, firm, organization, association, governmental entity or other legal entity.*** Then it went on to say: ***'Person' does NOT include an individual serving a sentence of imprisonment in a state or country correctional facility in this state or any other state or any federal correctional facility.***

Troy's conclusion: He is a prisoner of the State of Michigan, therefore he is not a person.

I use this simple illustration to highlight an issue that troubles me.

We talk about 39,000 people in the Michigan prison system, numbers of blacks, numbers of whites, numbers of reoffenders, numbers of women, numbers of seniors...heck, each prisoner has his/her own ID number, and that's how they're known. No names, just numbers.

We've dealt with a lack of humanity in prison statistics forever. But look at the rest of the news.

No one talks about gymnast Rachel Den Hollander. Instead, we lump together the incredibly large number of athletes who were sexually molested by Dr. Larry Nassar.

No one talks about geography teacher Scott Beigel, or his 14 year old student Gina Montalto. They are just among the sad number of casualties in the latest of many school shootings in this country.

In church, in the coffee shop, in our city council, in our state legislature, with our congressman and senators, and yes, with our president, we talk numbers. When we do that, we don't really have to dig below the surface to discover that these are, or were, tender, fragile human beings just like you and me.

Says St. Paul, in describing the body of Christ: ***...its members should have mutual concern for one another. If one part suffers, every part suffers with it; if one part is honored, every part rejoices with it.***

So when x-number of Michigan prisoners aren't getting adequate health care and inferior food, that includes Troy, but **we all suffer**. When x-number of athletes are abused by a physician/molester, that includes Rachel, but **we all suffer**. When families are torn apart as students like Gina and teachers like Scott get gunned down, **we all suffer**.

I was reading of a rape victim who used adversity to bring about change. "Mama Masika" committed her entire life to protecting and raising awareness of rape as a weapon of war in the Democratic Republic of Congo.

It's past time to react and respond.

On that day when all citizens join families and friends of inmates to support humane prison care, when men and women who are not affected by molesters stand with victims to demand change, when all US citizens join hands with Florida teenagers to hold our government accountable for mass shootings, **we all win!**

What we are called. Does it matter?
Saturday, January 20, 2018

Last year a member of a fine, protestant church responded to my request for support of the work of **HUMANITY FOR PRISONERS.** That would not be happening, he explained, because his church opted to spend mission funds on those agencies actually teaching the Word of God.

Also last year, as I sought the support and assistance of a highly capable agnostic, she stubbornly insisted that unless HFP become more secularized, it was doomed to failure.

Granted, the topic is a touchy one. When we appeal to churches for support, we refer to this as a ministry. When we appeal to secular foundations that want to avoid religion, we call it an advocacy agency.

And all this gets me to thinking. Somehow, we're missing the point. If we focus on the prisoner and his or her needs and problems, those issues fade in importance.

I'll give you a couple examples.

Thursday, Matt got up early in the morning to make the drive to Jackson so that he could be at the side of an ailing prisoner for his Parole Board review. One might ask why Matt did this. After all, the guy had violated parole once before, and he's known to be a bit of a con man. Well, here's why: The man had no friends or loved ones willing to accompany him for this traumatic experience, he's shown love and concern for dozens of other hurting prisoners, and besides all that, he's terminally ill! Cancer will claim his life within the year. It's where we belonged.

That same day, Volunteer Jennifer Juhasz and I went to the Muskegon Correctional Facility to meet with 12 prisoners who are hoping to file applications for commutation of their sentences. We did a free-wheeling two-hour workshop on how to fill out the forms. One might

28

ask why we did this. After all, the Governor has shown reluctance to grant any commutations so far. Well, here's why: The Governor will leave office by the end of the year, he may decide to show compassion to some deserving long-term inmates, and most importantly—it's a sliver of hope for those who long for freedom! It's where we belonged.

That's right. With 39,000 people in the state prison system, we spent all that time and effort on one inmate in Jackson, and 12 in Muskegon.

I must confess to the church man: Matt, Jen and I didn't take a Bible with us, and didn't mention Christianity once in those two sessions.

I must confess to the Agnostic: In both instances, we felt that this was what Jesus would do.

Ministry or agency. Does it matter?

What's the famous line of Shakespeare? *A rose by any other name would smell as sweet.*

Douger: They don't know what they're missing!
Wednesday, January 3, 2018

I was taken aback a couple of years ago when a consultant for HFP said, **no one is doing what you do**. And then he went on to say, **No one *wants* to do what you do!**

In retrospect, I don't know why that surprised me.

One time I was doing a review of my book **SWEET FREEDOM** with members of a Christian book club, and a couple of the people actually became hostile. I'm still not quite sure why that happened. Perhaps they just didn't like to hear about a white man trying to help a wrongly convicted black man.

I was invited to tell about our ministry to an adult class of a Christian Church one time, and only a handful showed up. Little to no interest in helping the "least of these," from those who, in my opinion, should have had the most interest.

Matt and I traveled to a lily-white city one day to speak to a group of businessmen in that city's major service club. Polite applause. Everyone made a quick exit. No words of thanks.

We recently put out an appeal hoping to find housing for an elderly black man battling cancer, who has no friends or relatives left, and who would like to die outside of prison. Very little response.

I had forgotten those words of our consultant until we received a neat message, including holiday greetings, from one of our friends behind bars: **You folks do a job that nobody else even wants to think about! For that I thank you all.**

One thing that's missing in all this narrative is how beautiful it is to work with the marginalized. Fr Greg Boyle:

30

"Compassion isn't just about feeling the pain of others; it's about bringing them in toward yourself. If we love what God loves, then, in compassion, margins get erased. 'Be compassionate as God is compassionate,' means the dismantling of barriers that exclude."

As we sit on the threshold of 2018, all of us at HUMANITY FOR PRISONERS—staff, directors, volunteers—boldly proclaim that we not only *want* to do this work. **We love it! We love the people with whom we work! Our lives are brighter because of these relationships!**

"We must not sit idly by as injustices abound around us. We have a voice and we must use it. We must advocate for those who no longer have a voice. We must love greatly."

— Dr. Christina Hibbert

31

March 29: Maundy Thursday; Maurice's birthday!
Wednesday, March 28, 2018

March 29, 1944: Birthdate of Maurice Henry Carter.

Interesting that this comes up during Holy Week. That Maurice's birthday actually falls on Maundy Thursday.

These days I think so much about the mother of Jesus. Just a few decades earlier she had given birth to this child under the most mysterious of circumstances. And now, to have it all come to an end under the most cruel of circumstances. Heart-breaking!

Maurice Carter's death was heart-breaking for his mother, as well.

Little black boy, born to a kind, Christian woman in Gary, Indiana, whose husband wasn't around any longer.

A nice little boy, always soft-spoken. Son of a single mom in an inner city neighborhood, their home next to a red-light-house, he managed to endear himself to the "ladies of the night." He was the polite young man who took their apparel to the dry cleaners for their generous tips and grateful words.

As with most young black man of that day and that area, he got into his share of scrapes and problems.

But he took pride in himself. Always dressed properly. Pleasant demeanor. No unkind words. Didn't descend into the pit of drugs, thievery, sex and debauchery.

Then came that fateful day in the Christmas season, 1973, when an off-duty police officer was shot and injured in downtown Benton Harbor. Maurice just happened to be in town that day with an acquaintance. One year later, that same "friend" turned into the jail-house snitch who told police that Maurice was the shooter.

The rest is history. The snitch recanted, but too late. Maurice was found guilty of assault with intent to commit murder and sentenced to life in prison: no weapon, no motive, no fingerprints, no evidence. A white cop was shot, and a black man was going to pay. Maurice paid with 29 years!

Back to his mom. When I came aboard, adopted Maurice as my brother and member of my family, and committed myself to obtaining his freedom, I also became a member of *his* family. I made certain that every Mother's Day and every Christmas I paid her a visit in Gary. How she would laugh when I reminded her that if Maurice was my brother, she was my mother!

I'm thinking of Jesus' mother this week.

I'm thinking of Maurice's mom, too.

Two mothers who dealt with more than their share of pain. Two mothers who knew their sons were not guilty.

Maurice Henry Carter: March 29, 1944—October 25, 2004.

RIP, Maurice.

Guess who I found behind bars!
Friday, December 29, 2017

A sad excuse for a human being was knocking on the door of a homeless shelter, probably hoping to find a place to sleep that night. Asked Father Greg Boyle of a fellow Jesuit priest who answered the door, "Who was it?" Answered the priest: ***Jesus in his least recognizable form.***

It was a profound reminder to me: **That's exactly who I see behind bars!**

Now don't give me that "soft on crime," "bleeding heart," "no concern for the victims" stuff. I'm an old man and I've been in this for years. I know darn well who's in prison and why.

But give me a little space to explain.

Yesterday, two stories crossed my desk. Some unpleasant prison staff members a couple weeks ago took every wheelchair from one medical unit in the women's prison, leaving crippled people weeping and begging, some crawling on the floor. Another officer shouted, "Get that woman off the floor!" In a day or two the wheelchairs were back again, but why did that happen?

On the same day, I received a message from an inmate who has every reason to be bitter. His application for commutation was denied. Honestly, I can think of no one more deserving of freedom. But instead of reflecting that anger, he told how he befriended a cynical old gang-banger who has been torturing and terrorizing inmates for years. He discovered that the man's birthday is approaching, collected some little items from friends, actually gift-wrapped them, and is planning a little birthday observance. He's hoping a little kindness will show the bad actor that there's a better way.

Which sounds more like Jesus to you?

34

We hear stories of kindness, compassion and just plain goodness regularly from behind bars.

- *A woman watching out for a dear old lady with dementia*

- *A man begging for us to help two geriatric patients who he thinks are dying*

- *Prisoners constantly asking us to help peers with special needs*

- *Musicians who do their best to enhance in-prison worship experiences*

- *Inmates who organize fund-raising efforts for charities on the outside*

- *Hobby craft participants knitting and crocheting goods for the homeless, poor and needy*

- *Horticulture experts growing vegetables and flowers for others*

Jesus said, *I was in prison and you visited **me**.*

I note that he didn't say, "*You visited some very unpleasant or evil person in prison.*" In my humble and "untheological" mind, I interpret that to mean that, when I enter those prison doors, hear the clanging of the gates behind me, and look out over the sea of faces (many of them of a different color), **I see the faces of Jesus.**

Perhaps the Jesuit priest would describe them as ***Jesus in his least recognizable form.***

At year's end, I thank God for this experience.

Prison visit: The gift that keeps on giving!
Wednesday, December 20, 2017

Bob got some bad news this week. His family won't be coming to visit him in prison. Family members are in Texas, and they claimed that some snow prevented their travel. The visit will have to be by phone for this Christmas.

He's taking it in stride. It's a way of life for prisoners.

Some years ago the Minnesota Department of Corrections conducted a major study on the impact of visitation. Said the experts: **Based on both statistic and anecdotal evidence, <u>visitation can be the difference between continuing a cycle of reoffending or finding hope to start a new life</u>, according to experts and research.**

And yet they don't get visits—

- *Retired Warden Mary Berghuis contends that only 12% of Michigan prisoners get visits*

- *HFP Prison Doctor Bob Bulten recently called on a long-time inmate. It marked the first time he had ever had a visit!*

- *My friend Jimmy has been in prison 18 years. He's never had a visit!*

A dear friend of ours, wife of a wrongly-convicted lifer, recently put out an appeal to friends and relatives of Michigan inmates: Make a prison visit! She told how bad weather forced cancellation of just one of her regular visits with her husband, and how much they both missed it.

Looking at from a selfish perspective, it can, indeed, be an annoyance. For one thing, it'll probably involve a long drive. Then there'll be the long time spent in the waiting room. You may have an unpleasant experience with a Corrections Officer.

But you couldn't make a better investment of time! Even though you can't bring in food, you can't bring in gifts, you CAN bring in yourself. Plan to buy him or her some food from the vending machines, take advantage of the photo op. Allow time. And don't think you have to do all the talking. These people have no one with whom they can just sit and share thoughts and experiences. They just want someone to listen.

I apologized to an inmate, once, because in a prison speaking engagement I didn't answer all of their questions very adequately. "Heck," he said, "most of the guys already knew the answers. They just wanted to be with you!" It was the visit that was important.

It's probably too late to do it before Christmas, but it's never too late.

Make it a part of your Advent/Christmas/holiday/New Year commitment.

I was in prison and you visited me! Jesus knew then, and knows now, the importance of the prison visit.

In this season of Advent, I long for his return.

Corrections Officers, It's time to step up to the plate!
Wednesday, December 6, 2017

Two short stories.

Donald's wife gives me a call. He's been in prison 42 years, he's 76 years of age, and he's been a model prisoner. A quiet, gentle black man, Donald never got tickets, never challenged authority, and was liked by peers and staff alike. He finally got an opportunity for parole...he was granted a Public Hearing before the Michigan Parole Board. We attended, and spoke up in his support. That was some months ago.

The reason for the call from Donald's wife: He was granted a parole! Good news! God be praised!

Then came the negative part of the story. **Following the Public Hearing the prisoner is housed in a holding area until a van can arrive, pick him up, and take him back to the facility where he resides. While in that holding area, a few nasty Corrections Officers choose to harass him, telling him he's never going to get out. "You'll die in here."**

Donald could hardly talk when he related that story to his wife that night...he broke down weeping.

Story Number Two.

Lisa is a 55 year old white woman, living in Michigan's only prison for women in Ypsilanti. Her words:

My two daughters came to visit this past weekend. The officer threatened one of them, saying that she could not wear altered clothing and told her she had to do a strip search to prove it, and if she was lying she'd never visit again. She took her, along with her 4-year-old daughter and her 7-year-old son into the visitors' bathroom and made my daughter strip in

front of the kids, all of whom were crying. Then, at the end, when they were leaving, the officer pointed at my younger daughter and her little boy, asking who she was to my older daughter. She responded, "My sister and nephew." The officer said, " Mmm, she likes her some black men...got her a black baby," about my 5-year-old grandson. My grandchildren never want to come see me again "where the bad people work."

I have to admit, many years ago when I got started in this business, I had a problem with all corrections officers. But, I've changed my mind! I have met many fine officers, men and women who do their very best under trying circumstances, who manage to stay kind and fair, and who gain the respect of prisoners and visitors. It's not an easy job under the best of circumstances.

However, this stuff is unacceptable. We can go on blaming the Warden, the MDOC and all the people at the top, but I'm thinking that it's time to start lower than that. I'm calling on all decent officers, and I'm calling on the Michigan Corrections Organization—the union that represents some 6,500 corrections workers—to take a stand.

The Union's web site says the organization is "leading a nationwide campaign to raise the professional profile of corrections officers."

It's time to deal with your own...time to intensify that campaign! Stories like this don't smell very good.

What's in the brown paper bag?
Wednesday, November 22, 2017

On this Thanksgiving Day, 2017, I'd like to share a beautiful story...a story not written by me. I feel certain that Luis Ramirez would be honored to have us pass along what he has written, but I can't ask him. He's dead.

This message came to me from Death Row in Texas a few years after our organization was formed. We hear a lot of stories about prisoners. As President of HFP, though, I think it's important for all of us to be reminded that prisoners are people, they have feelings and emotions, and as I understand it, all are created in the image of God.

Anyway, here's my Thanksgiving gift to you today...a story from the late Luiz Ramirez: (In all caps, just the way he sent it)

I CAME HERE IN MAY OF 1999...A TSUNAMI OF EMOTIONS AND THOUGHTS WERE GOING THROUGH MY MIND. I REMEMBER THE ONLY THINGS IN THE CELL WERE A MATTRESS, PILLOW, A COUPLE SHEETS, A PILLOW CASE, A ROLL OF TOILET PAPER AND A BLANKET. I REMEMBER SITTING THERE, UTTERLY LOST.

THE FIRST PERSON I MET THERE WAS NAPOLEON BEASLEY. BACK THEN, DEATH ROW PRISONERS STILL WORKED. HIS JOB WAS TO CLEAN UP THE WING AND HELP SERVE DURING MEAL TIMES. HE WAS WALKING AROUND SWEEPING THE POD IN THESE RIDICULOUS-LOOKING RUBBER BOOTS. HE CAME UP TO THE BARS OF THE CELL AND ASKED ME IF I WAS NEW. I TOLD HIM THAT I HAD JUST ARRIVED ON D.R. HE ASKED WHAT MY NAME IS. I TOLD HIM. HE HOLLERED AT EVERYONE: "THERE'S A NEW MAN HERE. HE JUST DROVE UP. HIS NAME IS LUIS RAMIREZ."

I DIDN'T KNOW WHAT TO MAKE OF IT. LIKE MOST OF YOU, I WAS UNDER THE IMPRESSION THAT EVERYONE ON D.R.

WAS EVIL. NOW THEY ALL KNEW MY NAME. I WAS SURE THEY WOULD SOON BEGIN HARASSING ME.

WELL, THAT'S NOT WHAT HAPPENED. AFTER SUPPER WAS SERVED, NAPOLEON WAS ONCE AGAIN SWEEPING THE FLOORS. AS HE PASSED MY CELL HE SWEPT A BROWN PAPER BAG INTO IT. I ASKED HIM, "WHAT'S THIS?" HE SAID FOR ME TO LOOK INSIDE, AND CONTINUED ON HIS WAY.

MAN I DIDN'T KNOW WHAT TO EXPECT. I CAREFULLY OPENED THE BAG. WHAT I FOUND WAS THE LAST THING I EVER EXPECTED TO FIND ON DEATH ROW, AND EVERYTHING I NEEDED. THE BAG CONTAINED SOME STAMPS, ENVELOPES, NOTE PAD, PEN, SOAP, SHAMPOO, TOOTHPASTE, TOOTH BRUSH, A PASTRY, A SODA, AND A COUPLE OF RAMEN NOODLES. I REMEMBER ASKING NAPOLEON WHERE THIS CAME FROM. HE TOLD ME THAT EVERYONE HAD PITCHED IN. I ASKED HIM TO FIND OUT WHO HAD CONTRIBUTED...I WANTED TO PAY THEM BACK. HE SAID, "IT'S NOT LIKE THAT. JUST REMEMBER THE NEXT TIME YOU SEE SOMEONE COMING HERE LIKE YOU, YOU PITCH IN SOMETHING."

I SAT THERE ON MY BUNK AND THOUGHT OF HOW MANY TIMES I HAD SEEN "GOOD PEOPLE" OF THE WORLD PASS BY SOME MAN, WOMAN OR CHILD HOLDING A SIGN THAT SAID HUNGRY, OR WILL WORK FOR FOOD. I'M GUILTY OF THE SAME. I JUST PASSED THEM BY. YET HERE ON DEATH ROW AMONG THE "WORST OF THE WORST," I DIDN'T HAVE TO HOLD UP A SIGN.

I NEVER GOT TO TELL NAPOLEON ABOUT MY FEELINGS. HE WAS EXECUTED. I COULDN'T FIND HIS FAMILY.

WHAT'S IN THE BROWN PAPER BAG? I FOUND CARING, KINDNESS, LOVE, HUMANITY AND COMPASSION ON A SCALE THAT I'VE NEVER SEEN THE "GOOD PEOPLE" IN THE FREE WORLD SHOW TOWARDS ONE ANOTHER.

After reading this story, I wanted to send a note of thanks to Luis Ramirez. But I was too late. He was executed by the state of Texas in October, 2005. He was 42. He claimed wrongful conviction until his death.

"What you do to these men, you do to God"
—Mother Teresa during her visit to San Quentin Prison

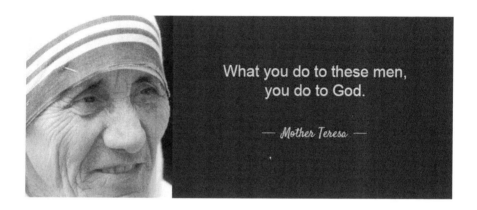

Two Fs that are NOT obscene: FOIA and First Amendment!
Sunday, September 17, 2017

Something very significant occurred recently in the City of Grand Rapids. The city was forced to release a series of audio recordings from the police department...recordings that were seriously damaging because they showed an obvious intent to give favorable treatment to an obviously drunk driver. The reason: the guy was an assistant prosecutor.

The significance, here, is not that they tried to go easy on somebody from the prosecutor's office, although that, too, is not to be disregarded. One can be sure that if you or I got stopped by the same cops, for the same infraction, nobody would be on some secret phone line trying to save our butts. No, the real significance here is that the information was obtained through **Michigan's Freedom of Information Act.**

MLive, publisher of the Grand Rapids Press, refused to take no for an answer, contending that "***the people have a right to know how government is acting on its behalf, how taxpayer dollars are being spent, and that good judgment is being exercised in a fair and transparent manner.***" MLive took this challenge all the way to the Michigan Court of Appeals, and the public was served.

I raise this issue to point out the fact that journalists are not the only ones making good use of the Freedom of Information Act. I don't think a week goes by that HFP doesn't file a FOIA request on behalf of someone in prison. We have a lawyer who counsels and advises us on these issues, and Matt has become adept at using this system, thus providing valuable assistance to many Michigan inmates.

But, and here's the rub, you cannot imagine the resistance to transparency. I have a friend who's an elected county official, and who boasts that the FOIA coordinator in his county—a retired lawyer—makes certain that the absolute minimum bit of information is released under provisions of the act. Witness how the City of Grand Rapids battled the Press, perhaps thinking that the extensive fights and legal costs would prod the newspaper into just dropping the issue. Matt constantly meets resistance and encounters delays, making one wonder just how much stuff is hidden in those records that officials don't want prisoners—or the public—to know!

As taxpayers and followers of HFP activities, I write this piece to remind you just how important this procedure is, but also to stress that it must be safeguarded against those who seem to like official secrets and believe the public does not have a right to know. Prosecutorial misconduct and the hiding of evidence can and do result in wrongful convictions.

A tip of the HFP hat to those courageous journalists who effectively pursue the truth through FOIA requests.

We're finding it a useful tool, also. And we're not going to back down, either!

That does it. Now we're mad!
Wednesday, September 13, 2017

It's no secret that we're declaring war on bad medical treatment and care in Michigan prisons. We'll do it in a calm, reasonable, and legal manner.

But sometimes, especially this week, when reading

- *That a guy gave specific symptoms of a torn retina last February, when the physician says there was a 90% chance of saving his vision, but because they waited so long they think he'll go blind...*

- *That a guy claimed he was having a heart attack, so they gave him Tums and sent him to his room, where he died of heart failure...*

- *That a woman with colon cancer who desperately needs surgery keeps getting postponements...*

- *That a prisoner with Crohn's Disease is unable to get an appropriate diet...*

- *That a prisoner with sleep apnea was ordered to ship his CPap home when he was booked in, and now cannot get another...*

- *That a woman in the infirmary is complaining that her sheets are "awful...almost gray and black..."*

- *That an inmate who suffered a torn ligament in his leg still cannot get treatment four years later...*

...I feel like the guy in the 1970s film *NETWORK*. He was the guy who got so fed up with particular issues until he

45

exploded: *I want you to get up right now. Sit up. Go to your windows. Open them and stick your head out and yell — 'I'm as mad as hell and I'm not gonna take this anymore!' Things have got to change. But first, you've gotta get mad!*

I promise to listen to our wonderful doctor, whose email messages continue to bear the beautiful, calm and insightful words from the founder of World Vision International: **May my heart be broken with the things that break the heart of God.**

But—and I'm not a theologian—I call it "righteous indignation," and we're *not gonna take this anymore! Things have got to change.*

No question about it: We're mad!

So are our doctors and lawyers.

A Reason to Celebrate!
Monday, July 24, 2017

Doubly blessed! That's what I think of on July 24.

In 1978, the newest member of our family arrived. Marcia and I were both 41 when Matthew Douglas was born. More than a decade had passed from the time we were heating baby bottles and changing diapers, and the other three kids were well along in life. Then came this dude.

As I've learned so many times in four-score years, there's a divine plan.

In an era when some unsettling business and personal matters could have been disastrous, the possibility of troublesome and harmful thoughts was completely offset by issues and events such as baseball cards, Tigers games and Saturday hot dog runs. Our other kids may have been growing up, but there was still a little guy waiting for his dad at suppertime, no matter how disturbing the day's events may have been at the office.

We've found that parents don't love one child more than another, but Matt did make his mark as the one who not only followed me into the radio broadcasting business, but later into the field of prisoner advocacy.

26 years after Matthew arrived on the scene, the next big July 24 event took place: Maurice Carter walked out of prison! He had served 29 years for a crime he did not commit. Ironically, Matt covered that very story as a newspaper reporter. It was this prisoner, and our mutual efforts to obtain his freedom, that steered me into a third career. Thanks to the late Maurice H. Carter there's an organization called HUMANITY FOR PRISONERS which is now touching the lives of hundreds of Michigan prisoners.

And so, on this July 24, I celebrate. A little white kid and an old black man, both of whom gave me some of my gray hairs; and both of whom—without a doubt—made an incredible impact on my life.

Happy Birthday, Matthew!

We'll meet again, Maurice!

Surprise. The Attorney General represents ALL of us!
Monday, July 17, 2017

I was trying to explain my frustration with the Michigan Attorney General to one of the newest members of our team.

We were talking about the Public Hearing, an essential step for a lifer before he/she can be granted parole or a commutation of sentence. The hearing is conducted by the Michigan Parole Board, but the activity is dominated by an Assistant Attorney General who mercilessly grills the inmate, who is under oath, not only about every minute detail of the crime, but also about what he/she was thinking at the time. The Assistant AG defends his actions, saying he is representing the "People of the State of Michigan." The meaning is clear: He represents the victims of the crime, and their families.

My complaint is that the family and friends of the prisoner are also members of the Michigan populace. He represents us, too, and while he may not realize it, sometimes the prisoner is actually the most damaged victim in this situation. I've had criticism of our work as prisoner advocates from people who ask, "What about the victim?" The assumption is that we are on different sides. It's "we" vs. "they."

And then my friend Holly, to whom I was venting, wisely put her finger on it: ***That's one of our major problems today.***

So true.

- Our President thinks America can go it alone.

- Votes on major issues in congress are strictly on party lines, the people be damned.

- It's important to get a majority of conservatives or liberals on the Supreme Court, because the other side is evil.

- It gets right down to the personal level. If you don't agree with me, you must not like me. Families are split, churches are split, communities are split.

It begs the simple question: Aren't we all in this together?

OK, off my soap box and back to prisoners. It should be incumbent on all of us to not only seek healing for victims of crime, but also to seek restorative justice, and healing and rehabilitation for the perpetrators of crime. Punishment, retribution and mass incarceration are getting us nowhere and costing us a fortune.

Said American historian Aberjhani: *There is no envy, jealousy, or hatred between the different colors of the rainbow. And no fear either. Because each one exists to make the others' love more beautiful.*

Said St. Paul in the book of Romans: *Let us therefore make every effort to do what leads to peace and to mutual edification.*

May it start with me.

50

The bad ones are in jail, and the good ones are not, right?
Monday, July 10, 2017

I have three questions for you. They'll come at the end of this blog.

The court appoints a **defense attorney** for an indigent black man, charged with assault with intent to commit murder. The <u>first time he meets with the defendant</u> is the morning of the trial. He fails to thoroughly cross-examine the single witness who insists the defendant is the wrong person. The jury buys the story of the Prosecutor, and the poor African American is sentenced to life in prison. Wrongly convicted.

A **County Prosecutor** <u>knowingly uses junk science</u> to convict a woman who has no prior offenses, is known to be a devout and upright person, whom witnesses claim could not have committed the crime of murder...but his boasts for continued re-election are that he has never lost a case. The victory was obviously more important to him. The woman is in for life. Wrongly convicted.

A **Circuit Court Judge** <u>refuses to listen to the testimony of professionals</u> in the field of psychiatry, and decides that a 13-year-old boy should be tried as an adult, and when convicted, sentences him to the state prison system. His mental illness has never been properly treated. He's been raped and abused. He's now in his 20s.

An **aggressive attorney** reads about a criminal conviction, and convinces a wrongly convicted inmate that with a down-stroke of $60,000, he can sue the pants off the lawyer who lost the case for him. The minute he gets the down payment, he cannot be found or contacted again. The money is gone. The man remains behind bars.

An **innovative attorney** sees and hears that prisoners are grasping for straws as Governor Snyder reaches his last year in office. They're hoping he'll grant some commutations of sentences, so this lawyer promises that, for a fee, he can file such an application better than anyone else. The record shows that the Governor has never granted one so far, except for medical reasons. The lawyer takes the money. The prisoner remains in his cell.

A **crooked lawyer** has been promising everything but the moon to men behind bars, but after he receives the down payment he fails to show up for meetings, claiming illness, and doesn't bother to answer his telephone. He won't even return critical legal documents. The money has vanished, and so has the attorney.

All of the people listed in bold print are home with friends and families this summer, enjoying outdoor barbecues, driving to work each day in nice cars, and telling society that our judicial system works. It's the best.

The people who were sold down the river never got out. They're hoping for visits from friends and family, dreaming that someday they might be lucky enough to attend an outdoor barbecue. When we hear from them, they're just wondering if anyone even cares.

OK, here are my questions:

- *Who, among the above, do you think belongs in prison?*

- *Do you care?*

- *What are you going to do about it?*

Happy Father's Day?
Saturday, June 17, 2017

I'm a dad who, but for the grace of God, could be observing Father's Day behind bars. I've been talking a lot about the wrongly convicted in recent days, perhaps because there have been a couple of high profile exonerations in the news. It's still on my mind.

As I write this blog on the evening before Father's Day, I'm sitting in my tiny office in the lower level of our modest condo. My little buddy hummingbird sips from a feeder that I have positioned outside the glass sliders. I'm having fun watching a kingfisher diving for fresh fish in the nearby pond out back. It could be different. I've never been in trouble with the law, but...

My friend Matt is a wrongly convicted businessman. He had never been in any trouble, either, until a tragic weekend when he got blamed for a crime that never even occurred. Some innovative police officers and an ambitious prosecutor changed this man's life forever. That was nine years ago. He'll be observing Father's Day in prison for four more years. His grown kids are out of state, so there'll be no visits this year.

My pal Anton is likely to be in prison for the rest of his life, unless the Innocence Project reviewing his case is able to turn things around. Anton has some learning disabilities and couldn't read or write when he was wrongly convicted. I'm convinced the bullying cops got him to sign a document which he couldn't read, and which turned out to be a confession. He was a teenager then. He has a daughter and a grandchild living in the inner city now. Once again this year, he'll have no visits on Father's Day.

For Harold it was a different story, and one that we've seen several times, where an aggressive prosecutor turns a tragic accident or a tragic suicide into accusations of a homicide. A legal team is hoping to undo the damage, but

53

this professional person suddenly found himself surrounded by armed officers, then was arrested, tried, convicted, and sentenced to life in prison. That was 17 years ago. His kids are grown now, but a daughter hasn't appreciated having an incarcerated dad and won't speak to him anymore. It won't be much of a Father's Day.

These are three true stories. With 2.2 million people in jail or prison in the United States, do you think they are isolated examples?

I pray for a special group of hurting dads this year...dads who are in prison, dads who have family members in prison, and dads who love their kids just as much as you and I do.

May they feel warm and loving hugs of the Heavenly Father.

There may not be much else.

On Wrongful Conviction Day, 2000 innocent people sit behind bars in Michigan! Do you care?

Sunday, October 1, 2017

The second of October marks the fourth observance of International Wrongful Conviction Day. I contend that it should be declared a holiday in this country. Not a fun holiday like Christmas, New Year's Day, Fourth of July or Thanksgiving Day. No, this would be a sad observance, like Memorial Day. Yes, there should be a nationwide effort calling attention to this dreadful infection in the body of what we call the judicial system.

Wrongful Conviction Day was organized to raise awareness of the causes and remedies of wrongful conviction and to recognize the tremendous personal, social, and emotional costs of wrongful conviction for innocent people and their families.

I'd like to call your attention to the **Innocence Network**, an affiliation of organizations dedicated to providing free legal and investigative services to individuals seeking to prove innocence of crimes for which they have been convicted, working to redress the causes of wrongful convictions, and supporting the exonerated after they are freed.

As you probably know, it was a wrongful conviction that got me into this business many years ago. As a result, HUMANITY FOR PRISONERS has always kept a strong focus on the topic. And for good reason.

4.1 percent of defendants who are <u>sentenced to death</u> in the United States are later shown to be innocent: 1 in 25, according to the Washington Post.

Time Magazine reports that, **for the third year in a row** the number of exonerations in the United States has hit a record high. A total of 166 wrongly convicted people whose convictions date as far back as 1964 were declared innocent in 2016. On average, there are now over **three exonerations per week**—more than double the rate in 2011!

There are no hard data re the number of wrongly convicted prisoners in our system, but estimates range between **5% and 15%**. Here in Michigan, that means there are probably **2,000** innocent people in our state prison system, and possibly as many as **6,000!**

Leading causes, as listed by the experts:

- Eyewitness Misidentification.
- Junk Science.
- False Confessions / Admissions.
- Prosecutorial Misconduct.
- Informants or Snitches.
- Bad Lawyering.

So take a moment today, not only to say a prayer for the victims of wrongful conviction and those working on their behalf, but also to support all efforts to reduce this problem.

After all, there's no guarantee that the next victim won't be you!

Prison guards need non-violent communication training, too!
Tuesday, April 25, 2017

It's a terrible thing to lose your mom. It's even worse for someone in prison to lose a mother, or any family member for that matter. There's no way to mourn. No one to talk to. There's no quiet time for reflection. Other family members can't be there with you to share memories. You may not even attend the memorial service. It's heart-wrenching!

So a young, 28-year-old Connor was hurting last week on the day of his mother's funeral, and it's no surprise that he got into an argument with a Corrections Officer. From that point on, specific details aren't available, but we've received enough reports that substantiate the final chapter of the story. Connor told the officer his mother had died, and the aggravated officer replied, "F*** your mom!"

Connor's response was a quick punch to the officer's face. And predictably, other guards raced to help and Connor became a punching bag. He was hauled away to Level 4 in a cart, we're told, bleeding and suffering from possible head injuries. Connor has now been transferred to a prison where they have a Level 5, which is tantamount to solitary confinement. His grandmother is worried, and we're trying to find out more.

It's easy for me to use a broad brush when painting a picture of Michigan prison guards, and I want to avoid that. I regularly meet very nice people behind bars who try hard, and do their best. It's not an easy job. Many prisoners live up to their reputation and make life miserable for these officers. And that leads me to my topic for today.

In recent years our former Board Chairman Dan Rooks and I have traveled to numerous prisons in the state to lead workshops. I talk about the services that HFP can and does provide, and Dan, who is a practicing clinical psychologist, talks about non-violent communication. In fact, Dan is so adamant in his determination to help prisoners with anger management that he teaches a course, twice a month, on that very topic in a state prison.

Every time he speaks, prisoners beg him to start a similar course in their facility. They take notes. In the noisy environment of the prison, you can hear a pin drop when Dan discusses alternatives to violent responses to provocation. The inmates seem like sponges, absorbing every drop of precious information on the subject.

In addition, I have seen prisoners take the initiative on this topic. In my two most recent visits to the Cotton CF in Jackson, I've witnessed hundreds of inmates taking a peace pledge...swearing to do their best to lower incidents of violence in their environment.

BUT, I've never heard of such a thing among corrections officers. And as I see it, this is a two-way street. If their union is already making work of providing non-violent communication skills to their members, God bless them. It's the route to go. If not, then such action is past due.

I'm not a violent person...dunno if I've ever hit anyone. But I can tell you this: You'd better watch out if you say to me, "F*** your mom!"

Belated Happy Birthday, Maurice, from the Detroit Police Chief!

Thursday, March 30, 2017

Maurice Carter would have been 73 years old yesterday. It's tradition that I put together some kind of a blog on his birthday.

March 29 came and went, and so did any ideas for the blog page. Then, at a minute before midnight, the Detroit News published a great story! The Police Chief of City of Detroit is going to put forth a major effort to slow down wrongful convictions. It's an article worth reading...a story that tells about Chief James Craig, and his meeting with Innocence Clinic people at the University of Michigan Law School. He pledged his full cooperation. This from a county whose system of justice has seemed seriously flawed over the years.

This is huge!

I say this because a lot starts with the cops. Let's go back to the Maurice Carter case.

It was action by crooked cops that got it all started in his case, and that led to Maurice spending 29 years behind bars for a crime he did not commit.

Maurice and a buddy were questioned shortly after an incident in Benton Harbor where an off-duty police officer was shot and injured, while shopping with his wife in a downtown store. The policeman was white. The shooter was black. They paraded him in front of the store so that the clerk could try to identify him. She insisted that Maurice was not the assailant...wasn't even the same color black.

Two years later, it was crooked cops who persuaded Maurice's buddy—who was facing drug charges—that if he told some lies about Maurice his charges would be reduced.

He agreed to sign a statement claiming he saw Maurice running from the scene of the crime. And that led to his arrest and eventual conviction.

True, there were other typical factors in this wrongful conviction: faulty eye-witness identification, and the testimony of a jail-house snitch. But it all began with some police officers with tunnel vision; officers who (in my humble opinion) knew who the real perp was, but were determined to put this outsider in jail. Maurice was from Gary, Indiana, and had no ties to Benton Harbor or Michigan.

For those who are not familiar with the story, Carter was never exonerated. I was privileged to lead a fight seeking his freedom for the final decade of his life. We ultimately obtained a compassionate release, because of serious illness. Maurice walked out of the Duane L. Waters prison hospital in July of 2004. He died exactly three months later.

But today, in the aftermath of his birthday, we can celebrate the fact that a prominent Michigan Police Chief has not only made an important decision, but is doing so in a high profile manner that may encourage others in law enforcement to take similar stands.

Maurice would be pleased.

Not much peace around these days, but I saw some in prison!

Saturday, March 25, 2017

Many, many years ago, when our kids were little, the piano tuner was in our house struggling to get our little baby grand up to pitch. I say struggle, because Marcia had her hands full. The kids were chasing, then fighting, and then one started crying. It was Christmas time. The tuner muttered, "Peace on earth, good will toward men."

I'm remembering that incident late on a Saturday night. I've just returned from the G. Robert Cotton Correctional Facility, one of several state prisons located in Jackson. Former board chairman Dan Rooks and I were there as featured speakers today, guests of their Chance for Life Chapter

To set the stage for my comments, I perhaps should make brief reference to this week's happenings.

On the International level, another terrorist attack...Isis taking credit.

On the national level, a stunning defeat in Washington that left not only Republicans fighting Democrats, but Republicans fighting with each other.

On the state level, many constituents this week had been fighting with their congressmen.

On the local level, residents are fighting mad over how to handle the over-population of deer in our city.

In church circles, I'm aware of people so angry about the style of music in their worship that they're thinking of making a switch.

It wouldn't be appropriate to discuss personal issues, but I'm aware that some of our friends are in the midst of personal battles.

Not much peace. At any level.

In the midst of that, I drive to Jackson on a cloudy, rainy, cold day. And here's what I find: 200 men—different races, different backgrounds, different faiths—gathered in an assembly, hoping to launch a <u>6-month</u> peace initiative!

Last summer I was privileged to the deliver the keynote address at this same prison, when a group of men pledged to harness what they called the Divine Force of Peace for one month. The results in the prison were amazing. And so this time, the Chance for Life Chapter decided to go for a six-month stretch. Six months, for men serving time in prison, to restrain from fighting, bullying, arguing and causing problems...six months to see the other guy's point of view, stressing forgiveness, kindness and compassion.

Before I was introduced, one of the leaders—explaining this dream, this goal—stated that as of today, more than 600 men have already signed the pledge! 600 men who are convinced that if peace starts with them, there's no telling where it will spread.

Think we could learn from them?

I do. I did.

I may not even need a sermon tomorrow. Their testimony was a divine message, and I thank God for their initiative and their courage.

Holiday obits, especially painful for prisoners!
Tuesday, December 27, 2016

The loss of family members and loved ones seems more painful when death occurs in holiday seasons. My only sister was killed by a drunk driver at Thanksgiving time. Marcia's dad died at Christmas time. My father died when we were welcoming a New Year. In my humble opinion, though, the pain seems worse when it must be suffered alone.

I'm mindful of that during this week between Christmas Day and New Year's Day, because people are hurting as the result of two recent deaths in my circle of friends. I invite you to note the dramatic differences between these two stories.

My good friend Fred Groen died on December 17. He was a charter member of HIS MEN, the Christian male chorus that I founded in 1972, and that I directed for 21 years. Fred was one of only three charter members still actively involved in the ensemble. He failed to recover from critical heart surgery, after struggling in the hospital for three months. BUT, he and his wife Bev were able to discuss all possibilities before he underwent surgery, she was able to be at his bedside during the torturous 90 day period, all family members were able to be in Holland at the time of his passing to console and comfort each other, and a beautiful memorial service was staged in his home church including three touching presentations by HIS MEN. Beautiful.

Now for a story of contrast.

My good friend Mark lost his mother on Christmas Eve. Mark is in prison on a wrongful conviction. He's from the state of New York, and that's where his mother and step-father lived. She was failing both mentally and physically, and the family knew that the end was near. But no one could be near Mark at this difficult time. And he wasn't able to be at her bedside in her final hours. He had to hear about his mother's passing by telephone. The closest thing to family and friends are his classmates in a Calvin College program where he is enrolled in Ionia...a relationship that has been terribly important right now. When we chatted today, he wanted to talk about his mom. "She was the only constant in my life," he said. "From the day I was born until the day she died, she was there for me, she believed in me, and even when health was failing she visited whenever possible."

Mark cannot attend a memorial service. Family and friends can't surround him with memories, hugs and condolences. He's behind bars. At the very least, we're going to do our best to see if he can get permission to watch a video of the memorial service. But even that is not a sure thing.

Grief is no discriminator of persons. May God grant comfort to members of both families.

As I reflect on this today, I'm so grateful that walls and bars and barbed wire cannot hinder or stall or prevent the peace that passes all understanding.

Is there a "reason for the season" when you're in prison?
Thursday, December 22, 2016

MEMO TO MY DEAR FRIENDS BEHIND BARS:

I always struggle at this time of the year, wondering what kind of wishes I could send your way. It seems just plain wrong to wish you "Happy Holidays," when I'm fully aware of the conditions around you.

I know you won't receive gifts, I know you'll receive few if any greeting cards. If statistics are correct, there's a good chance that you won't get a Christmas visit. The many and varied reports that we have received over the years regarding holiday meals haven't been good. There's no reason to believe your Christmas dinner will be any better this year.

While I completely understand why this is possibly not a pleasant time for you, I'd like to encourage you to take a second look. I contend "the reason for the season" has importance specifically for YOU!

I got thinking about this last Sunday, when our pastor pointed out the difference between the words "sympathy" and "empathy."

You see, I can have sympathy for you, because I'm saddened that you must exist under these conditions.

But this Jesus, whose birth we celebrate in December, has empathy for you because he can personally identify with all of your issues, all of your struggles. To quote an overused and overworked statement, he's "been there and done that."

Think you were born under unpleasant conditions? His parents were virtually homeless when it came time for Mary to give birth. Someone finally made

space in what, today, would probably be considered a garage.

Have family and friends pretty much abandoned you since your incarceration? He was despised and rejected by his own people.

Did the so-called "justice system" treat you unfairly? His trial was a mockery.

Were you wrongly convicted? He was not only wrongly convicted, but wrongly executed.

Having trouble forgiving yourself for the crime that put you there? That's why he came.

Thinking that this might be the last chapter in your life, and you didn't want it to end this way? That's why he came.

That's Jesus, whose birthday I encourage you to join with me in celebrating. Yep, actually celebrating! It may seem like no one else cares for those behind bars, (although *I do!*), but we have every assurance that **he cares!**

His words: *He has sent me to proclaim freedom for the prisoners.*

Saying it on Facebook isn't enough!
Saturday, December 17, 2016

So you want to put Christ back into Christmas, do you? I keep seeing your indignant messages on Facebook, so I'm assuming you must mean it.

But first, we must figure out who this Jesus Christ really is. We can't focus on a cute little baby in a manger, tended by a glowing mother, receiving gifts from important foreigners, and lullabied to sleep by singing angels. The very beginning of life for Jesus was tainted by uncaring people who refused to help the homeless, and it didn't get any better for the next 33 years. He was ridiculed, mocked, scorned, abused—rejected by his own—and eventually wrongly convicted and executed.

That's the Christ you want to put back into Christmas?

The one who, when handed a scroll while teaching in the synagogue in Nazareth, said: ***The Spirit of the Lord is on me, because he has anointed me to proclaim good news to the poor. He has sent me to proclaim freedom for the prisoners and recovery of sight for the blind, to set the oppressed free...?*** The one who, when telling a parable, actually put himself behind bars when he said: ***I was in prison and you visited me.*** That Christ?

It seems to me that if you mean what you say, it might be time to

- befriend a prisoner, with visits, letters and cards (unconditionally, no strings attached)

- do what you can to help a prisoner's family during this difficult time

- offer your support to a prison ministry not only with prayers, but with dollar

- persuade your church that mission fields are not only in foreign lands

- personally communicate with your state and federal legislators regarding such subjects as prison reform and mass incarceration.

Walking the walk, that's the key. Not just talking the talk.

Then, I believe, the Christ, who we put back into Christmas, will say, **whatever you did for one of the least of these brothers (and sisters) of mine, you did for me.**

Post-election nausea? Not in prison!
Thursday, November 17, 2016

It may surprise you to know that some prisoners aren't really all that anxious about the state of national affairs.

The appointment of a white supremacist to a key position in the White House may seem like a national disaster to you. But frankly, David is more concerned about his bowel movements. He's a paraplegic, and the only way he can go is with the assistance of personal medical care…something he doesn't always get in the prison hospital. Then he has accidents.

A national election that is decided by the Electoral College, rather than a popular vote, may be spoiling your appetite these days, but Cary has spent more than $100,000 on attorneys to prove his innocence, and all he has to show for it is receipts. They didn't give him what he paid for. No more money. No freedom.

Words of hatred and bigotry not only dominate our TV shows, but are even showing up in our social and religious circles. But I must tell you that all of this disgusting behavior is not what's on Nathan's mind. He has been diagnosed with cancer, he's in the Michigan prison system and gets no indication at all that doctors plan to do anything about it.

As a spouse and a parent, you may find **shameful talk and descriptions of women** by public officials to be totally unacceptable. But Cindy, who was an award-winning professional before she was arrested for killing her habitually abusive husband as he tried to kill her, couldn't care less. She has already served 12 years of a life sentence for what an aggressive Prosecutor called *First Degree Murder*. Says Cindy: "The judicial system that I believed to be fair and just has betrayed me." She questions whether she'll ever be free again.

The fact that a national candidate who advocated for **free college education** lost the race for the Presidency may bother you, but it's of no concern to Tony. He just appeared before a member of the Michigan Parole Board, hoping to get a positive review...and when he shared with her his dream that, if released, he wanted to go to college...*she laughed at him!*

I'm not saying we shouldn't be concerned about the topsy-turvy national picture right now. There'd be something wrong with us if we weren't. But it's important to keep things in balance. The world is different in prison, and our issues aren't necessarily theirs. One prisoner wrote: ***Being in prison is worse than death. At least when you're dead the pain stops. The life you once knew <u>is no more</u>. You can see it, but you can no longer interact with it. You're trapped in a monotonous limbo watching time march on for your loved ones. But for you, it does not.***

These are the people with whom Matt and I are holding hands on a daily basis, following strict orders from Jesus to just show a little compassion and kindness. Their problems, perhaps small by comparison to some in our minds, are huge to them.

In all of the controversy of the moment, please do not forget us or them.

More than ever before, HFP and our prisoners need you: your prayers and your support.

When prisoners wish time stood still
Thursday, October 6, 2016

So the sun stood still, and the moon stopped, till the nation avenged itself on its enemies,... The sun stopped in the middle of the sky and delayed going down about a full day.

—Joshua 10:13.

I'm sure we've all had experiences where we wished time would simply stand still.

I clearly remember a time in my life when my world was crashing all around me, and I was about to lose my business...a business I loved. Marcia and I had taken a short getaway in Florida before everything came to an end. On our last day there, as I stood alone on the end of a dock, I wished time would stand still. I didn't want to face the music.

Let me explain the reason for this blog...it all stems from a recent prison visit.

I was part of a group of three who went to prison not only to discuss business, but to just share love and concern with a prisoner who has been wrongly convicted. Having spent more than 15 years behind bars for something he didn't do, Mr. D treasures visits like these.

And while there, observant reporter that I am, I watched some other scenes.

I saw a daddy in prison blues playing with his little son, not much more than 2 years old. It was a tender scene. The little boy was good. His mother was patient and kind. But his dad couldn't get enough of the toddler. Playing with him. Carrying him. Walking, hand-in-hand, around the room.

71

I saw a young couple obviously in love. Somehow, I don't think they were married. The young man didn't look like a criminal. And his girl-friend wasn't the kind of floozy that you might think would be frequenting prisons...she was classy, attractive, and well-dressed. They were starry-eyed. There were enraptured gazes and bubbling conversations.

Somehow, I think Mr. D wanted this time with his friends to stand still. I honestly believe that the young father wanted time with his little boy to stand still. I'm convinced the young man whose lover came to cheer him up never wanted to stop looking into her eyes.

But that's not the way it is in prison. Friends, family and loved are forced to leave. Prisoners who experience the joy of visits are harshly ushered back into reality by undergoing the humiliating mandatory strip search before returning to their rooms. And, unlike in Joshua's time, the day comes to an end.

Prisoners aren't statistics, they aren't an inmate number. They are real people with real faces and real names. Their feelings and emotions are no different than yours and mine.

Just one short experience in the visiting room and your life will never be the same.

I started with a verse from the Bible, and I'll end with another. Thankfully, all prisoners, and all of their loved ones, can look forward to this day:

He will wipe every tear from their eyes, and there will be no more death or sorrow or crying or pain. All these things are gone forever.
—Revelation 21:4

Reading anything about former prisoners doing good?
Me neither.

Thursday, September 29, 2016

Marcia and I were watching the news, as a reporter explained that the man who committed this particular crime had recently been released from prison. That's the kind of stuff that makes the news, and that's the kind of stuff that sets back possibilities of parole for many others. We have no hard data to support this, but all of us involved in this kind of work are convinced that this negative publicity just stiffens the position of the Michigan Parole Board. It gets tougher for worthy inmates to catch a parole.

I'll be the first to admit that, even in our small organization we've been stung. People who we thought were good immediately resumed doing bad things the moment they got out. But the story that seems to get missed by the media (and I tread lightly here, because I was a part of the media for nearly 30 years and I felt that my reporting was very balanced) is the wonderful story of second-chance successes by ex-offenders.

This whole topic is fresh in my mind because this week Matt and I had a very productive luncheon meeting with a couple leaders of **70 X 7 LIFE RECOVERY OF MUSKEGON**. We were talking about the reluctance of Christians in general and some churches in particular to accept ex-offenders, let alone welcome them. "When that happens," said Executive Director Joe Whalen, "we just turn Nate on them!"

70x7
MUSKEGON
JOB ANCHORED REENTRY • RECOVERY • RESTORATION

73

Nate Johnson is now the Mentoring Director for this fine agency, explaining the importance of second chances to parolees. And when he speaks to a church group, people listen. You see, as a teenager, he was among the most 'successful' crack cocaine dealers in Muskegon. He was arrested at 19, received a lengthy prison term. The big story here is that he made life-altering good choices while serving that sentence. He has successfully re-entered the Muskegon community and now helps to touch lives of those who traveled down similar roads.

I don't remember reading any headlines about Nate's amazing story.

And there are so many others; so many with whom we've worked who are now productive citizens, not only grateful for their freedom, but anxious to convert that earlier negative into a future positive! We have a file full of beautiful stories of men and women who screwed up, but made a conscious decision to change. Today they are more than paying their debts to society. I'm not reading or hearing much about it in the media.

All of us can tell stories about second chances. My name is at the top of list. A second chance with endangered health; a second chance after a lot of mess-ups (for which, thank God, I did not get arrested!).

Yours and mine may not be newsworthy. But, the comeback tales of many Michigan prisoners are exceptional and worthy of media attention.

These "second-chance" people are worthy of a welcome in your neighborhood, too.

And your church.

The worst of the worst? I don't think so!
Sunday, August 28, 2016

Former Director of the Michigan Department of Corrections Dan Heyns once referred to the people housed in our state prison system as "the worst of the worst!" I chided him on that, and he later recanted, in a private email to me.

I wish Dan Heyns had been with me Saturday. A group of guys in the G. Robert Cotton Correctional Facility in Jackson, all part of a positive and exciting project called Chance for Life, were concluding a month-long emphasis on peace. And we're not just talking world peace here. The focus of their Peace Initiative got right down to personal peace, peace between each other, and peace between inmates and staff.

It was a day of guest speeches and special recognition. I was honored to deliver the keynote speech. But that's not the reason for my desire to have Heyns there. Before my speech, as the program got underway, one of the presiding inmates read this statement about respecting diversity: *The concept of diversity encompasses acceptance and respect. It means understanding that each individual is unique, and recognizing our individual differences. These can be along the dimensions of race, ethnicity, gender, sexual orientation, social-economic status, age, physical ability, religious and political beliefs, or other ideologies.*

Then, as I sat there waiting to be introduced, more than 150 men representing many of these differences recited a peace pledge. Each man had been carrying this little card all month. As they recited the words they inserted their own name. They promised to seek peace in their own lives, to resolve conflicts in a peaceful manner, to respect the opinions of all others, to actively work at ending violence.

The worst of the worst? I don't think so.

My thoughts couldn't leave that pledge during the long drive home. I was the high and mighty speaker, focusing on the St. Francis Peace Prayer, but could I have signed that pledge?

I could just hear myself:

I can live by that pledge—

Except when I discuss politics—then it's my way or the highway when it comes to topics like presidential candidates, immigration, and guns;

Except when I talk about church—then it's my way or the highway when it comes to topics like gay marriage or style of music;

Except when I'm driving, as I stomp on the accelerator refusing to let some nut job cut in front of me.

Do you see what I'm getting at, here? Politics at the highest level has never been so stinky. Road rage is at an all-time high. We use documents like the U.S. Constitution and the Holy Bible to justify intolerance. Bullying, at lowest grade levels, is a problem in our schools. I think we can learn from the 150 guys I met with Saturday.

Those guys get it, and they not only get it, they're determined to keep this Peace Initiative going beyond the month of August. They're committed to ending violence, respecting diversity and celebrating human development.

Said the Apostle Paul, in the book of Romans: *If it is possible, as far as it depends on you, live at peace with everyone.*

I'm thinking that some people behind bars, incorrectly labeled the "worst of the worst," have a pretty good head start over many of us on the outside when it comes to efforts toward peace.

Michelle didn't deserve this!
Thursday, August 18, 2016

I'm going to share a sad story with you today. It comes from my friend Linda, who is a prisoner here in the State of Michigan. Normally, before we publish stories like this, we tweak them, brush them up, rearrange them, to make them look and sound nice. Not so this time. I'm going to let the narrative take its erratic path so that you can actually hear the sobbing hiccups, feel the dampness of the tears.

Linda tells the story of a fellow prisoner named Michelle, who is no longer with us.

I have been in this unit since April 11. Michelle went to diabetic lines every morning and evening. I never knew Michelle as a healthy woman. For these few months, every time a health care professional walked through the waiting room, Michelle asked, "please help me, when am I going to be seen, I hurt so much." I worked in the medical profession for several years, and in that time I have never seen edema as bad as hers. Her legs were not only swollen, but as her leg rested against the side of her wheelchair on the way to diabetic lines, the compressed, indentation remained through her entire wait. She had bed sores on her body that she could not reach and needed another inmate's assistance to apply ointment to them. But what the tragedy of this is, she was yelled at by officers, ignored by nurses and doctors and called a faker. One particular officer, on more than one occasion, yelled at her, yelled loud enough to be heard 5 rooms away through closed doors, that she was faking and could not use the wheelchair in the unit. "Get out of that chair, you're faking and going to really need it if you don't get up and start walking!" Michelle pleaded, "I can't, I hurt, you don't understand how bad I hurt." One day she fell in the bathroom, nurses came in to the unit and the unit officer told them she didn't need a gurney, that she was only faking it.

This week Michelle died. Do you know why Michelle died? Her cancer of the stomach returned, aggressively, and took her without any time left to treat or even give her the humanity of care and kindness that she deserved. She was ridiculed and left to suffer and ignored until the new PC came into the unit and sent her to the infirmary. She finally got sent to the hospital, but it was too late. She had no time left.

My immediate response: I should call a doctor. (I did.) I should call a lawyer. (I did.) I should tip off the media. (I did.) But there's only so much that Matt and I can do. We continue to hear stories about mistreatment of women by the State of Michigan, and yet nothing seems to get done.

So here's my suggestion this time: Share the story. Share it with any Michigan taxpayer you know. Share it with your State Senator and your State Representative. Complain loudly. Make your voice heard.

I have no idea as to the nature of Michelle's crime, if there really was one. I have no idea whether she was a problem patient. I do know this: She was someone's daughter; she was created in the image of God; and, she did nothing to deserve this kind of treatment.

The good news is that Michelle is in a better place now, where there's no pain, and no more tears are being shed.

The bad news is that we're still weeping here.

Mother's Day prayers for battered moms
Sunday, May 8, 2016

Mother's Day isn't a day of gladness and reunion for everyone.

For example, it's a day of sadness for those who have recently lost mothers, a sad day for those women who want to be mothers but cannot bear children, a day of regret for those mothers who mistreated their kids and wish they could live their lives over again, a day of painful memories for those who chose abortion and now wish they hadn't.

But today, I want to focus on an even smaller group of women. Some of them are mothers. Some perhaps would have been mothers under different circumstances. They're in prison for killing or seriously injuring their spouse or significant other, a deadly climax to years of violence and abuse.

I'm especially mindful of that, in the quiet of my office on this Mother's Day morning, because I have two friends who the state has determined should spend the rest of their lives behind bars. These women are not hardened criminals. They don't have a history of violence and illegal activity. To the contrary, they are well-educated and could be considered professional in their fields.

Here's a typical scenario that puts a woman like this in a prison cell and leaves her there. She lives with a husband who, to the public, may look like a pillar of the community, but in private abuses his wife, both physically and emotionally. She is shamed by this, hides it from her friends, takes much of the blame for this fearing that she is the problem in this relationship, and she even comes to his defense if authorities step in, because she might not have place to go and perhaps has no means of support if he were to be arrested. And so the situation continues and ferments until there's a breaking point...when she cannot take it anymore, and cares not about the consequences. She takes things into her own hands and brings an end to this abuse.

Prosecutors can be quick to call this first degree murder, claiming it was premeditated. In many cases, jurors haven't been allowed to hear about the years of domestic violence that preceded this heinous act. And if there's a conviction on first degree, there's an automatic sentence of life without parole.

I should point out a couple of things.

Number one, statistics show that women who kill men receive significantly higher sentences than men who kill women. And number two, approximately 90% of women who kill men are victims of abuse.

There's no quick answer here. HFP is partnering with some other professionals on a project that will shed more light on the subject, and offer alternatives, especially to prison sentences.

But for now, on this Mother's Day, 2016, I simply want to suggest that we keep all victims of domestic abuse, both inside and outside of prison, in our prayers. On a personal level, to my friends, Ms. L and Ms. N, I want you to know that you are in my prayers. This all began last night, as I listened to Lynda Randle remind me, in song, that the **God of the mountain is still God in the valley**. May you experience his peace today.

I'm offering my prayer in the name of Jesus, who not only showed love and tenderness toward his own mother, but who loves them all...especially those in prison.

Score one for religious freedom!
Friday, March 18, 2016

It happens so often. A problem is perceived, and as a result, a new rule is created. We have a feeling that's what happened in Michigan's prison for women, located in Ypsilanti.

According to our sources in the Michigan Department of Corrections, the prison warden wanted to make sure that the dayrooms, where prisoners gather during down times, weren't used for religious services which, under a specific corrections policy, are to be held in specific areas in the prison. And so a rule was created, and this is the exact wording:

IX. DAY/GROOMING/TV ROOMS

6. All religious studies must be done in your cell or at specified times in programs.

Armed with that new rule, Corrections Officers began immediate enforcement. One of our friends immediately contacted the HFP office: *"**We can no longer do Bible studies outside our cell. We cannot bring our Bibles into the dayroom and read them, discussing with our fellow believers. We can only wait for church services once a week, or read them in our rooms. For example, if I do not understand something while reading the Bible and I want to talk to my friend about it, it is against the rules, and I will get a ticket if I do so.**"*

We have learned to check out reports like this. We don't want to respond to the prisoner's complaint until we know it is valid, and we don't want to spread unfounded rumors. Sometimes prisoners are mistaken, or Corrections Officers exaggerate. Not so this time.

HFP went right to the top, checking in with one of our excellent and reasonable contacts in the front office of the MDOC in Lansing. An administrative aide confirmed the new rule, but added, *"...the intent was never to prevent prisoners from carrying their Bible to the dayroom or discussing religious matters with a fellow prisoner."* Then came the important final words: *"**To avoid confusion, the rule will be rescinded.**"*

Score one for religious freedom! This affects not only Christians, but adherents of all faiths—Muslims, Jews, Buddhists, Native Americans. And if this policy is firm in Lansing, it means that similar rules will not crop up in other Michigan prisons.

HFP—just doing its job!

A wedding behind bars, and I loved it!
Friday, February 19, 2016

I participated in a wedding ceremony today. I was the best man, the maid of honor, the ring bearer, and the official witness! In other words, there were only three of us standing before the presiding pastor. But I'm pleased to report that, as of 10:20 this morning, Jeff and Lena are husband and wife. He is a resident of the Earnest C. Brooks Correctional Facility in Muskegon; she is a citizen of Australia.

Matthew and I were brought into their lives by Jeff's prison roommate, a long-time friend, last November. Lena was coming to America and was hoping to find some legal assistance to pursue Jeff's claim of wrongful conviction. I met with her, viewed the network broadcast of 48 Hours that focused on this case, and put her in touch with Attorney Marla Mitchell-Cichon, Director of the Cooley Law School/WMU Innocence Project. Two things happened. The Innocence Project took the case, and we became very good friends with Jeff and Lena. So, it was no surprise when I was asked to witness the wedding. I readily accepted.

As one might expect, the State of Michigan and more specifically the Michigan Department of Corrections didn't make it easy for the love-struck couple.

May we choose the pastor who will marry us? **No, the Chaplain will make that choice.**

May we have the wedding ceremony at noon? **No, the pastor we have chosen has a conflicting funeral service, so the wedding must take place at 10 AM.**

That's very close to the 10:30 count time. Could we have it at 9 o'clock, so that there will be a brief time for pictures? **No, the 10 o'clock time is firm. The pictures will have to be taken later in the day during visiting hours.**

As a simple act of kindness, would the department waive the cost for one wedding picture as a gift? **No. You must pay for all photographs.**

We have asked our friend Doug Tjapkes to be a witness. He's not on Jeff's visitor list but he has clergy status. **The warden has approved his presence, but only for the ceremony.**

May we have our picture taken with him? **No. The warden has not granted him permission for a photograph.**

If he may not wear street clothes, could we make an exception to prison policy just this once, and allow Jeff to wear a regular shirt for the ceremony and the pictures? **No. He'll wear prison blues.**

Against all odds, however, the brief ceremony was beautiful. The setting was the visitor's room in Brooks, and the only musical accompaniment was the hum of nearby vending machines. The Rev. Charles Poole, an elderly black pastor, presided with a smile on his face and kindness in his heart. The couple recited the vows that they had previously written and memorized for the event. Of all weddings in which I have participated, I have not heard more meaningful pledges of love and fidelity. I mumbled a blessing over the rings before that particular ceremony, and Jeff and Lena were declared husband and wife. All within 10 minutes!

I don't ever recall getting teary-eyed at a wedding, not even those of our kids. Today my life, my heart, my tear ducts were touched by this warm experience behind the cold bars of a Michigan prison.

My favorite theologian, Frederick Buechner, has this to say about tears:

...of this you can be sure. Whenever you find tears in your eyes, especially unexpected tears, it is well to pay the closest attention. They are not only telling you something about the secret of who you are, but more often than not God is speaking to you...

May God extend his grace, peace and mercy, in abundant measure, on this couple.

They'll need every bit of it.

Do you get the picture?
Tuesday, February 9, 2016

It was a rather strange and unique scene at one of Michigan's prisons in Jackson yesterday. There sat an old white man, wearing a Christian clerical collar, beside an aging black man in prison blues, a practicing Buddhist. The occasion was a video session with a member of the Michigan Parole Board. I was making the case for a parole for this man, who has now served 25 years behind bars.

First, I should explain how I came to know this prisoner.

"Hey Mix, take a picture of us."

I was in the visiting room of the Thumb Correctional Facility many years ago, visiting my dear friend Maurice Carter. In those days, if you purchased a ticket for a couple bucks, you could have a photographer take a picture with you and your friend, standing against a wall at the end of the room where a mural had been posted. Maurice always enjoyed having our picture taken.

Mr. Mix was another old-timer in the prison system, and he was in charge of the Polaroid Camera. He was always polite, but seldom uttered a word. One day, as I was leaving, he stepped up, shook my hand, and thanked me for what I was doing on behalf of Maurice.

I forgot all about that kind gesture for years, and then, while waking up one morning, I got to wondering. I wondered if Mix was still in prison, and I wondered if he'd still remember me. I checked the inmate listings...he was a lifer, and still there. I sent him an email and a letter, thanking him for those kind words years ago. And I sent him a copy of the book SWEET FREEDOM, which tells the Maurice Carter story.

And thus my friendship with Mr. Mix gained momentum. We remained in contact over the years, and recently we learned that he was getting his first meeting with a member of the Michigan Parole Board. He would become eligible for parole this spring.

The inmate, now 62, has a grown daughter in Detroit, and four grandchildren he has never seen. He's a good man, and deserves to get a fresh start. Even though he was permitted to have a representative for the Parole Board interview, no friends or family members were available. I would be there.

I explained to the Parole Board member that, at age 79, I don't get up very early on a winter morning and make a two-hour drive in the dark just for the fun of it. I was there to support a release for the inmate, and I believed he needed a second chance.

I suppose there are those in the Christian community who question this style of witnessing. No Bible study, no prayers together.

Mr. Mix simply threw his arms around me and thanked me for this act of kindness. A prayer for the success of this meeting came later, in my car.

I think Maurice was pleased.

I think Jesus was, too.

If Jimmy is a friend, just imagine how Michigan treats its enemies!

Sunday, January 17, 2016

My friend Jimmy is a Michigan prisoner. Ironically, among prisoners, he's probably one of the state's best friends.

In 1989 he cooperated with law enforcement officials in the investigation of a bribery with the Michigan Department of Corrections. Charges were filed, and there were convictions on the state and federal levels, including corrections officials.

Since that time he has continued to provide law enforcement with information leading to numerous arrests for offenses such as auto theft, stolen property, and a multi-million dollar phone fraud scheme with the MDOC. The information that he has provided has also resulted in the recovery of substantial quantities of narcotics, the arrest of several Detroit area fugitives, and the resolution of a Detroit homicide.

10 years ago he played a key role in the arrest and conviction of a murderer.

One would think that, with all of this wonderful cooperation with the good guys, the State of Michigan would do its best to take care of Jimmy.

Well, in all fairness, the state did offer to get him re-sentenced so that he might receive credit for time served (now 29 years!), as a thank you for his help in a major criminal case. But, after they got the conviction they wanted, they backed off on the offer. Now they can't seem to remember that they ever made such a promise.

Worse than that, the state has failed to provide the necessary protection for their witness and informant who is still living in the general prison population. With all of this baggage, Jimmy has a target on his back. Over the years we have tried to help. We were able to pair him up with a fine attorney with a known reputation as a fighter, and he hasn't disappointed. But the state wouldn't budge.

Just a couple years ago, someone tried to poison him. He became very sick, but he survived. We intensified our efforts.

Recently we assisted in seeking a commutation of his sentence, with a high-powered application. Attached to the form was a three-page letter <u>from the Assistant Prosecutor who originally tried his case!</u> He said that he's never done this before, and he'll never do it again, but he asked for the Governor's commutation of Jimmy's sentence. Quoting from his letter: ***...when one considers all the facts and circumstances of this particular case, i.e.:***

...the actual circumstances of the sentence offense

...Mr. J's age and attitude (he's now 62)

...the lengthy period of incarceration already served

...the ends of justice being served through his cooperation and testimony...

...the price that he has paid for such cooperation,

that the public good in this extraordinary case would be well served by commutation of Mr. J's sentence.

No soap. Our Governor denied the request. And guess what? Now he's in the hospital again. 10 days ago two thugs entered his cell while he was alone, intent on inflicting serious pain. Before it was all over, Jimmy was slashed above the eye, and as he tried to fend off the attacker, he received cuts of the hand and arm. He fell during the assault, his back slammed against a bunk, and he suffered possible back injuries.

Once again Jimmy survived...until the next time.

A devout believer, he feels that God is protecting him.

That's certainly more than the state is doing. Not a very nice way to treat a special friend!

A prisoner prayer - for the New Year
Wednesday, December 30, 2015

Lord of the universe, as we end one year and begin another, we ask that you hear our pleas on behalf of those behind bars.

Prisoners will lose loved ones in the year to come. Even though they will not be privileged to experience the physical closeness of friends and family in their time of grief, we pray that they may not only feel your presence, but also your comfort and your peace.

We know of your compassion for those whose minds were troubled. We know how, in Bible times, evil spirits were ordered to depart from the bodies of the mentally challenged. As we look to the new year, we ask you to do the same for those **troubled souls behind bars** who are not able to think clearly and respond correctly. In addition, halt those inmates and staff members who would harm them or do further damage. Instead, cloak their caregivers in a garment of compassion and concern.

Lord Jesus, may the **women behind bars** feel the same warmth and love that you showed to your dear mother, and friends Mary and Martha. In 2016, we pray that the women in our prison may be granted their personal, private space in a facility where conditions now are seriously overcrowded. May fellow inmates be tolerant of each other in these difficult times. May staff members reach a new level of sensitivity and kindness. May administrators climb to new heights to improve conditions for women in prison. In the new year, may these women receive more than enough personal hygiene products, more than enough hot water, and may their lives be brightened by friendly caregivers and sparkling clean showers.

May **elderly prisoners** escape from the fear of personal attacks in prison next year. Place a shield of protection around the sex offenders, the geriatric lifers, and the mentally challenged misfits. Protect them from persecution and attack by predators and gang-bangers, but also from abusive guards and staff members.

You know that the vast majority, perhaps up to 90%, of inmates will **not receive a visit** this year. May more kind people than ever before take a moment to visit a prisoner, and where there are no human visits, may *your* presence be felt in those lonely cells.

Your presence is needed in those cells, Lord. As we begin the new year there are **those whose families have either passed on or moved on**, and are now alone. There are **those who can no longer be convinced that the courts are just**, and can find no hope. There are those who have done their best, **who deserve to be released**, who have served their time, and still cannot even generate any interest. And then there are **those who remain angry and troubled**, who lash out at fellow inmates and staff, cause problems because they can, and have no qualms about hurting others. Calm their minds and their souls. Divert their plans to traffic in alcohol, drugs and sex. Help them to see that there's a better way than that of the gangs, and that there is no superior race.

It's not easy to be sick or injured in prison, and we ask that you remember **those with medical and physical concerns** today. Where there is pain, grant relief when medication may be scarce or non-existent. Where there is suffering, bless not only the inmate but also the caregivers. In this new year, give all medical personnel in our prisons a generous measure of understanding and compassion.

There are **many behind bars who love you**, Lord. They spend time thinking of you, speaking with you, and praising your name in worship. Protect them from persecution and ridicule. Wrap them in your everlasting arms. Help them, also, to avoid ridiculing and condemning those whose beliefs are different.

93

And for **those of us on the outside**, give us the insight to see that placing young people in adult prisons, excessive sentences, death penalties, mass incarceration, and the use of solitary confinement do nothing to reduce crime, but instead make existing problems even worse. We ask your specific new-year blessing not only on the **prisoners**, but also their **families and loved ones**, those **entrusted to care** for them, and those **people and agencies advocating** for them.

We close this prayer claiming your promises and believing that your miracles continue to occur, and can even take place in this dark and bleak environment. In fact, we pray for them in the year to come.

Hear our prayer, O Lord!

Amen!

Dirk was right!
Friday, December 11, 2015

Many people aren't all that interested in making life a little better for prisoners. It goes back to the old saying, "If they hadn't done the crime they wouldn't be doing the time."

Video producer Dirk Wierenga quickly made that discovery, as he started doing interviews for a new HUMANITY FOR PRISONERS documentary. A theme on improving the lot of prisoners was not going to work. If his video production was going to help us raise money, it would have to change direction. As he adjusted the focus of the documentary, Wierenga took the approach that 90% of these prisoners are going to return to society someday. They're going to move into our neighborhoods, work in our businesses, and attend our churches. If they come out with a positive attitude, having been treated with compassion while behind bars, 1) there'll be less chance of re-offending; 2) there'll be a strong chance that they'll be good neighbors; and 3), chances are they'll want to give back to society.

I'm convinced Dirk is right on both issues. I'll give some examples in just a second here as to how prisoners, even before they get out, want to give back. And I'm hoping that, when people see and hear our story through the video, they'll get it...they'll see that it's just plain common sense to treat prisoners fairly and with compassion.

Here are examples of how inmates are going far out of their way just to give back to society, even before they return to the streets.

We have boxes of warm kids hats, mittens and scarves, made by the women at Huron Valley to be sold in a charity store as a fund-raiser for HFP.

We have beautiful prayer shawls, knitted by the women, for our Prayer Shawl Ministry, where we send a shawl to the hurting loved one of a prisoner.

The men at one Michigan prison are knitting and crocheting items at an incredible rate for a homeless veterans' shelter in Northern Michigan.

One of our friends makes hundreds of teddy bears in an atmosphere almost like a small factory, to be supplied to the Graham Crusade and other worthy causes.

The men at Brooks CF in Muskegon knit warm head-wear for needy kids in a program called Kaps for Kids.

A group of inmates has asked HFP to help in getting patterns for sleeping bags and mats from an Ohio prison, because they want to make these items for homeless people in Michigan.

And that's just the tip of the iceberg. There are programs like these throughout the Michigan prison system. Granted, there are gang-bangers. Granted, some inmates are preying on the elderly and those convicted of sex crimes. Granted, some are still pushing guards down the stairs, or selling booze and drugs, or running their con games. But many want to change, and give back.

That's why we say it's important to treat them with kindness now. We want to develop an attitude that will carry through into the free world.

That's what the new video—**to a better life**—is trying to convey.

Dirk was right.

This is why I shed tears
Tuesday, October 20, 2015

I was sitting in the front row.

Some 100 people had gathered in the meeting room of the Unitarian Universalist Church of Greater Lansing. Michigan State University Drama Professor Lisa Biggs had put together a group of actors from the university, the church and the community, in order to present a stage reading of some excerpts from JUSTICE FOR MAURICE HENRY CARTER. This is the powerful and moving drama, written by award-winning Toronto playwrights Donald Molnar and Alicia Payne, which tells the story of my friendship with Maurice. For those few who may still not be aware of his plight, Maurice served 29 years in the Michigan prison system for a crime he did not commit.

This was not the first time I had heard parts of the play. Marcia and I were privileged to hear the first reading in a small room on the second floor of a Toronto theatre in 2008. Since that time we have heard actors telling the Maurice Carter story in many venues. Perhaps the most meaningful was a stage reading inside the prison walls of the Earnest C. Brooks Correctional Facility in Muskegon. A group of thespians in an organization called Shakespeare Behind Bars worked for a year on the production before presenting it to a small audience, including Marcia, me, some of our Board members and some special friends.

Sorry I'm getting so wordy here, but I just wanted to explain that the East Lansing experience last Sunday wasn't my first rodeo.

It was near the conclusion when something most unexpected occurred: I started weeping. I was listening to the lines about Maurice Carter eventually being freed on a compassionate release because he was terminally ill. He was enjoying his freedom. He met his mother outside of prison for the first time in nearly 30 years. He was

97

savoring the taste of a real hamburger, prepared on an open grille. I didn't realize the tears were flowing until I touched my face. My cheeks were wet. What the...!!! I'd heard these lines many times before. What was the big deal?

And I've been thinking about it since then.

I'm deciding that it wasn't just the memory of that glorious day, that wondrous event. It wasn't just the fine presentation by this group of non-professional actors. It was the bigger picture that was getting to me. You see, since that day I've been working with prisoners around the clock, 7 days a week, 365 days a year. I've discovered that my previous two occupations were merely preparation by God for this calling.

These are the things that make me weep:

Wrongful convictions are still a ho-hum way of life in our country, unless you happen to be the victim, or the family member of the victim, or the loved one of the victim.

It is still no easier to overturn a wrongful conviction! Witness the huge case backlogs of every Innocence Project in the United States.

The factors that placed Maurice Carter behind bars are still high on the list of WC causes: jail-house snitches, faulty eye-witness testimony, tunnel-vision police work and prosecutorial misconduct.

There is no let-up in the inhumane treatment of prisoners! The lack of appropriate medical care that led to the death of Maurice is still evident in every prison system.

It is still far too easy to get in, and far too difficult to get out! Prosecutors continue to refuse re-opening old cases. Judges continue to reject legitimate appeals. Parole Boards continue to demand confessions and demonstrations of remorse, and inmates refuse to meet those demands because they're not guilty.

The list goes on and on.

It makes me weep, and I think it makes Jesus weep.

It should make you weep, also.

Wrongful Conviction—It can happen to you!
Friday, October 2, 2015

It was a wrongful conviction case that got me into this business. Radio broadcasting, my first and greatest love, was luring me back after a 20-year hiatus. But then I met Maurice Carter, an indigent black man from Gary, Indiana, sitting in a Michigan prison and claiming innocence. That was in 1995. The rest is history.

Until that time, naïve newsman that I was, I felt that prosecutors just wouldn't get a warrant, an arrest and seek a conviction if they didn't really have a case. Little did I know.

Today is **Wrongful Conviction Day**, being observed on an international basis. The event was first organized by the Association in Defence of the Wrongly Convicted (that's the Canadian way to spell defense), based in Toronto and founded by former welterweight champ Rubin Hurricane Carter. I frequently hear people say that all prisoners claim they are innocent. Rubin Hurricane, on the other hand, told me when he was in Michigan drawing attention to the Maurice Carter case: "When you hear a prisoner say he's innocent, and he sticks with that story the whole time he's in prison, you'd better listen!"

Since that time, I have listened. And I want to tell you something, as we observe this special day. We hear the stories like those of Maurice Carter, and somehow we get the impression that it's usually the poor, black people who usually wind up wrongly convicted...they have no funds for proper legal representation and they encounter racial bias among jurists and jurors. While some of that is definitely true, the bigger truth is *IT CAN HAPPEN TO YOU!*

I can tell you horror stories of wrongful convictions of a doctor, a lawyer, a cop, a banker, a businessman, a teacher...all of them white, and all of them with the means to hire good legal representation. Yet, each of these people

100

found themselves behind bars for a decade before adequate proof was established that they had done nothing wrong! In a couple of cases, the innocent inmate died without exoneration.

There's a special way that you can observe this day in Michigan. Your state legislature is currently considering a bill that would compensate people who have been wrongly convicted. You can make sure that your legislator votes for this bill, and you can keep an eye on Pure Michigan to ensure that these victims of wrongful conviction are promptly compensated without years and years of red tape wrangling.

Aside from that, join me in a prayer today for justice in our system, especially for those wrongly incarcerated.

Quoting the writer of Proverbs: *It is not good...to deprive the innocent of justice.*

Who's gonna help these women?
Saturday, September 12, 2015

In California, they're reducing the number of prisoners. But it took a Federal Court order to get the ball rolling. Is that what it's going to take in Michigan? Nothing else has worked so far.

Michigan's terribly overcrowded prison for women has been a best-kept secret by government and corrections officials. We're going to do our part to change that.

All female state inmates are housed in one prison: Women's Huron Valley Facility, in Ypsilanti. There are actually two facilities in one, and together they currently hold approximately 2,200 inmates, and corrections officials told me last week that the number is going up.

The reasons why the women's prison population is increasing are worthy of a story, but we'll save that for another time. For now, we want to discuss the many ways women's rights are being violated by the state prison system due to this overcrowded situation.

Our office is being inundated by complaints from prisoners, and we've been in this business long enough to know that these aren't the "whiney-complainey" type people who always have a bitch. These are our friends—nice, common-sense people who are trying to make the best of their situation.

The American Friends Service Committee, a national Quaker organization, has a fine chapter here in Michigan. After a lengthy investigation into this overcrowding business in Ypsilanti, the Michigan office last summer sent a strong four-page letter to the corrections department, state legislators, and even a copy to Governor Snyder. I don't know whether they ever received a reply, but I do know that the letter did no good. Zilch!

One year later, and reports are flooding into our office—

- **women have no place to sit**
- **women have no room in their crowded cells**
- **women have absolutely no privacy—ever**
- **bunks moved into closets**
- **bunks moved into TV rooms**
- **bunks moved into activity rooms**
- **some of these rooms have no windows**
- **many of these rooms have poor circulation**
- **some are infested with ants**
- **some have leaky roofs**
- **overcrowding problems make staff irritable**
- **irritated staff members write more tickets**
- **visitation by friends and family is affected.**

In other words, it's a living hell in there. It's to the women's credit that they haven't revolted, not that anyone would listen or care.

I'm in the process of preparing a front page for our October newsletter with actual quotes from prisoners and family members at Huron Valley. I hope it gets widely distributed. I pray that it gets some action.

It appears the new prison administration, our Governor and our state legislature have no plans to bring about change. And if that is the case, perhaps it's time to go to the courts. I wonder which civil rights attorney would have the guts to start a class action suit for these deserving women?

God's children, created in his image, shamefully stacked like cord-wood in Pure Michigan.

It's time for action.

You can bet on it: We'll be there!
Wednesday, August 26, 2015

Supporters of HFP have every reason to join with the followers of Jesus who, in Matthew 25, said, "'When did we see you sick or in prison and go to visit you?"

I bring up the issue because for one of the few times in history, we made budget this month thanks to the kindness and generosity of people who believe in what we do.

I want to assure them, and assure you—

We'll be there for the woman whose colostomy bag must be replaced, but who has been told she may have new supplies on September 6.

We'll be there for he mother who has been denied access to her son, and hasn't spoken to him in over a year.

We'll be there for the guy whose wheelchair broke and the prison wouldn't give him a replacement.

We'll be there for the blind woman who is taunted by guards singing "Three Blind Mice."

We'll be there for the woman dying of cancer, who simply wants to spend her final hours surrounded by loved ones.

We'll be there for the lifer who will not be granted surgery until it becomes an "emergency."

We'll be there for the visually impaired who loves to read and simply wants a pair of reading glasses.

We'll be there for the mentally ill woman who was hog-tied because she disobeyed orders that she didn't even understand.

We'll be there for the inmate with learning disabilities who signed a confession that meant nothing to him, because he could not read or write.

We'll be there for the inmate who needs help filling out his commutation form because his spelling is so bad.

We'll be there for the hearing impaired who wants a hearing aid just so she can hear the instructions from her officers.

We'll be there for the old gent roughed up by the Parole Board for not remembering the details of his crime, simply because it occurred during an alcohol blackout.

The friends and parents and spouses and loved ones and yes, the inmates, can keep on adding to this list. It could go on and on. Because, thanks to your generosity, we'll be there!

The reply of the King: **I will tell you the truth, whatever you did for one of the least of these brothers (and sisters) of mine, you did for me.**

An empty chair at the memorial service
Monday, July 13, 2015

Michelle's teen-aged son will be buried today. The boy's father and grandparents will be there. His mother will be absent.

I cannot begin to describe my emotions: heartbreak, anger, disgust. And I don't even know Michelle!

Here's the story in a nutshell.

Our office received a message last week from the mother of a prisoner at the Women's Huron Valley facility in Ypsilanti. Her friend Michelle, age 44, learned that her 18-year-old son Josh had died unexpectedly at home due to an asthma attack. A death in the family is a serious problem for prisoners...something, we believe, that must be improved in the future.

We followed the situation day by day, here's the way it developed.

On the 7th, the day after the young man died, she was informed that she could be transported to the funeral home in the thumb area, accompanied by two officers, but she and her family would have to pay the tab: $1,000 each way.

On the 10th, we received a message that Michelle had found two off-duty officers willing to make the trip with her.

Then, **later that same day**, came this message: The officers who were going to help Michelle have been mandated by the prison to work their regular shifts at the prison on Monday. She won't be able to go. Her friends in the prison are showering her with love and sympathy.

I have difficulty accepting defeat, so I got up early this morning, summarized all of these messages, and fired off an email to one of our friends in the front office of the MDOC to ask if there was any way this grieving mother could still say farewell to her son at the 3 PM memorial service today. And here is the response, verbatim:

I worked on this case most of Friday and unfortunately, we won't be able to transport her today. These funeral visits are based on the approval of the warden (which was received) and the availability of two trained staff members on voluntary overtime. While one volunteer was located, the other volunteers could not be cleared for this assignment because they are on mandated overtime at the facility today. As I'm sure you've heard, the facility is utilizing a significant amount of overtime right now because of our ongoing CO vacancies and as a result, it is difficult to find staff that are both eligible and willing to take voluntary overtime. While we ultimately had 3 staff people volunteer for the assignment, 2 could not be assigned because they were called in for mandated overtime today. We simply don't have the staff available to complete the funeral visit today, despite the best efforts of the family and the facility.

The name of our organization is HUMANITY FOR PRISONERS. Giving our agency the name is one thing, but actually achieving humanity for prisoners is still another. It's easy to issue statements and cite policy. It's still another to hold the hand of a grieving mom.

I'm frustrated. I'm angry. I'm a parent and a grandparent. I'm hurting for Michelle. I don't know the answers, but I'm ashamed that my state couldn't do better than this. I find this completely unacceptable.

Thank God for the dear friends of Michelle behind bars who remain at her side. May our Heavenly Father grant her peace in this difficult time, and enfold her in his everlasting arms.

Just another day? Not in a heart-beat!
Tuesday, June 30, 2015

It was a religious experience! That's the only way I can describe it. And there were only five people in attendance.

Let me explain.

As a full-time advocate for prisoners, I savor the opportunity to witness that rare occasion when an inmate steps into the free world. My friend Joe Evans was due to be released from prison after 39 years behind bars. He has been serving a life sentence for a dastardly crime committed in his youth while high on drugs and alcohol. Now, he's a changed man.

Sensing that this might be a very special occasion, I invited videographer Dirk Wierenga to join with me. Dirk is producing a professional documentary about the work and the mission of HUMANITY FOR PRISONERS. We were not disappointed.

The location for this little program was 3100 Cooper Street, Jackson, Michigan...right at the front door of the Cooper Street Correctional Facility.

Joe is 61 now...his elderly mom and his cousin, who served as their driver, were on hand from the Detroit area to pick him up and take him home.

The prelude for this service is a discussion with a corrections officer at the front desk, who doesn't have any idea what the inmate's name is...he just knows his ID number. And his main concern is that Dirk isn't carrying any telephone or photography equipment into the prison. Other than that, he has little interest in the proceedings.

And then Part One of the ceremony: Joe is warmly welcomed by his mother and his cousin.

Part Two (the one I particularly enjoy!): Doug Tjapkes holds open the front door of the prison, as this dear man who spent two thirds of his life in prison, takes his first steps into freedom.

Part Three (which even tops Part Two!): Joe puts down his footlocker containing all of his earthly possessions, and throws his arms around Doug, tears streaming down his face. The bear hug seems to last forever. There's really no rush. Words of thanks and gratitude and love.

Part Four: When that hug is completed, Joe's mother is next in line for a hugging session with Doug.

Part Five: Joe is eloquent in this thanks to HUMANITY FOR PRISONERS for our part in helping him to obtain this parole. For the past five years we have been communicating, providing materials when necessary, holding his hand during health problems, speaking on his behalf in a Public Hearing, and finally welcoming him into society. "HUMANITY FOR PRISONERS is like the Red Cross for us in there," says Joe. "You are there to help when there's no one else."

Part Six: Sweet departure, as Joe and his little family leave Jackson for home, a home-cooked meal, and a good-night's sleep in a soft bed with lights out and sound turned off.

Said Dirk: "It was a special day...one I will never forget!"

Back to my opening statement: It was a religious experience! No hymns were sung, there was no sermon, the only prayers uttered were silent ones, and the congregation totaled 5.

Jesus was there.

The world ain't supposed to be that way!
Thursday, June 18, 2015

I've never forgotten the quote, although I have forgotten the circumstances. A preacher was quoting these words, emitted by an African American man, at the scene of a tragic inner city incident...using them as a sermon illustration. I remember those words, daily, as we hear one sad story after another in the HFP office. Let me share.

I was on the phone for a lengthy conversation with the elderly mother of an inmate yesterday. Her son was in good health when he entered prison, but two years ago an accident happened in the weight room. Another inmate dropped a 45-pound weight on his foot. X-rays showed no broken bones. That was two years ago, but the foot kept swelling. Later the swelling extended up to the knee. Three surgeries later, the swelling now extends to the groin. Doctors claim they don't know what it is, and can do no more. The inmate must wear what is called a pressure boot to keep his leg from swelling, and he's on crutches. The man is penniless. The elderly parents are on Social Security and have no means to retain expensive lawyers or doctors. Will the swelling go higher yet? Everyone can do nothing more than wring hands and pray. ***The world ain't supposed to be that way!***

An elderly dude sent a short letter to us: "I'm an 83 year old man with a bone-crippling disease and they won't give me any pain medication and they won't send me to the hospital for help. I'm in a wheelchair but healthcare won't allow me to have the chair to go back and forth to the medical line. I am confined to my room because they won't let me have the chair to move around. Will you please help me to get to a prison that can help me?" ***The world ain't supposed to be that way!***

A Detroit attorney tells how she tried to visit a mentally ill female inmate at the Huron Valley facility in Ypsilanti recently...a visit that had been previously arranged. She arrived with the inmate's mother at 4 PM. At 5:15 they were called into the visiting room where they waited some more. At 5:30 they were told the inmate refused to visit with them. The attorney explained to prison officials that the woman didn't have the option to refuse a legal visit because her guardian, who has the power to make such a decision, had determined that she needed this visit. By that time the word was that the inmate was back in acute care, and there could be no visit. Said the attorney: "It's hard to know what portion of this is intentional and what portion is incompetence. Regardless, the effect is a complete denial of access to counsel/the courts/family/legal guardian." ***The world ain't supposed to be that way!***

Makes me long for glory.

But for now, major prison reform cannot come soon enough!

Remembering prison moms today
Sunday, May 10, 2015

Mothers of prisoners

There are 43,000 people housed in the Michigan prison system this morning. All of them had a mom at one time...many of them still have a mother today. To these precious and hurting souls, we pay tribute on Mother's Day.

Many of the mothers will not see their offspring today, for various reasons (fewer than 15% of prisoners get any visits at all!).

- *The state has placed many of the prisoners in facilities too far away to make visits possible.*

- *Many of the mothers are elderly and/or incapacitated, preventing travel and visits.*

- *Some are estranged—the kids have no desire to see them, or they now have no use for their kids.*

- *Some have gone home to glory, not living long enough to see their child in a free society again.*

And among those who are fortunate and able to make a visit today—

- *Many are struggling with guilt: "If only I had been a better mother," or "If only I had paid attention to the early signs of mental illness," or "If only I had worked harder to keep a father in the family." I know this for certain, because I speak with you, I see the feelings of guilt in your eyes.*

- *Many are just struggling with shame and sadness. I see it in the visitor's lounge when you fail to make eye contact with me, a stranger in your midst.*

114

Moms in prison

There are 2,000 women in the Michigan prison system. Many are mothers. Many of these mothers won't see their offspring today, either. Statistics say that fewer than 300 will probably receive visitors.

- Their families are too far away...the drive to Ypsilanti is just too long.

- *Some of the kids are too young.*

- *Some are not only mother-less, but fatherless, and are being cared for by grandparents or friends.*

- *Some have grown kids who are ashamed of their mom, and don't ever want to see her again.*

- *Some have burned bridges, and are hurting with this loss of a relationship.*

- *Some have no idea where their husbands and kids have gone.*

The above lists are just samples...just the beginning. Each mother can add another reason to these lists or another variety on the same theme.

So when offering prayers for moms today, I simply ask that you remember mothers of prisoners and moms in prison. Many of them will not be remembered. Many feel forgotten. All are hurting.

To all of them we offer this Mother's Day gift: God's amazing grace. Our prayer is that each one feels God's peace and love today, regardless of all other circumstances. And we offer this prayer in the name of Jesus, who not only loved his own mom, but loves every mother!

From God's unending bag of surprises
Friday, April 3, 2015

Things like this continue to surprise me, even though, by now, I should be getting used to the most unusual ways God works.

This is the story of two wrongly convicted prisoners, from two different worlds.

Ed is 70, black, and not highly educated.

Mark is 20 years younger, white, and highly educated.

I met them both in the year 2009. Edward was in a remote location in the Upper Peninsula. Mark was in a Muskegon prison, right near our home. Both had compelling stories, and neither belonged behind bars.

Ed was blessed to have the assistance of Toronto-based AIDWYC, the Association in Defence of the Wrongly Convicted. (Yes, that's the way they spell defense in Canada.) But, due to alleged insurance issues, the AIDWYC trustees decided that the organization would no longer handle cases outside of that country. Ed was devastated. He had been clinging to that hope for eventual freedom. I am not an attorney, and HFP does not take on cases of wrongful conviction. The best I could do was to console him, pray for him, and try to find someone else to help.

Eventually, he got transferred. You guessed it: to Muskegon. That was in the fall of 2012. Now the two were in the same facility.

I put a bug in Mark's ear: See if you can do something to help this guy.

Mark, a recent graduate from Prison Fellowship's fine TUMI seminary program, did more than that. He virtually adopted the man! He helped organize all of his legal papers.

He wrote briefs for him. He helped Ed apply to Innocence Projects. And now, God be praised, it appears that a fine IP is keenly interested! There's new hope for Ed!

Ed can wonder why he ever got transferred to Muskegon, Mark can wonder why God allowed him to go to prison in the first place, both can wonder why I ever introduced them to each other, and I can go on wondering just how many times God is going to use this 78-year-old crooked stick to make things happen in the lives of prisoners.

Isn't this just like God?

Especially during Holy Week, we shouldn't be all that surprised.

Holy Week, not all that nice for many prisoners
Monday, March 30, 2015

I live in a broken world. Many of my friends are behind bars, and for many of them life isn't all that great.

While visiting in a Muskegon prison last night, one guy came to me to thank me for trying to help, even though I had done absolutely no good. He has torn something in his leg, and so he hobbles along in pain. Not only can he not get adequate pain medication, he can't persuade anyone to approve the necessary surgery to repair this injury. God knows we tried, all the way to the regional prison doctor and the warden of the facility. I don't know what else to do for the guy but to pray.

During the prison service last night I sat next to a man I've been trying to help for years. Other than finding him an attorney who cares and who is now working on his case, I have done very little for him. His conscience has dictated some activity in prison that has been very beneficial to law enforcement. In fact, he was promised that if he testified in a court case, efforts would be made to have him re-sentenced so that he would be able to see freedom. Well, he provided the necessary testimony and the state got a conviction. But, the state then reneged on its promise. Years later, he's still wondering when he'll get that hope for freedom. I don't know what else to do for the guy but to pray.

This morning I received an email message from a man I know in another Michigan facility. He just received divorce papers. Needless to say, relationships are more than difficult to maintain when one partner is in prison. I love the man. I love his wife. I don't know what else to do for the guy but to pray.

All of this is on my mind on the Monday morning of Holy Week...a time when we remember that our Lord

118

experienced the worst injustice of all, and eventually was wrongly convicted and executed.

It's in his name that I'll be praying for these friends and many more this week.

I know he'll understand.

For Black History Month: A tribute to 3 blacks who colored my life!
Thursday, February 19, 2015

Mattie Davis

In 1954, this little Dutch teenager began his first part-time radio job at station WMUS in Muskegon. To this point in my life, I had attended an all-white Dutch church and an all-white private Dutch school. Imagine the culture shock each Sunday morning when I expected to unlock the front door of the radio station to let in the singers of a black gospel quartet called the Heavenly Echoes.

The manager of this all-male ensemble was a dynamite little African American woman named Sister Mattie Davis. One of my first lessons from her involved prayer. I was used to all the Christian clichés that I had heard in my circles all of my life. Not so when Sister Mattie Davis offered her prayer on the radio every Sunday morning. Despite serious racist issues back in the 50s, she would earnestly plead for the safe-keeping of first responders: "the policemens and the firemens!"

Sister Mattie Davis, and her prayers, touched my life.

Cy Young

In the early 1970s someone contacted me at my radio station, WGHN in Grand Haven, and asked if I would like a guest on my talk show in observance of Black History Week (It was only a week back in the 70s). I quickly agreed, and a towering, handsome black dude showed up driving a car that looked like an accident waiting to happen. He introduced himself as Cy Young, former entertainer and emcee, now a pastor. He claimed to have the gift of recitation, and had memorized all of Dr. Martin Luther King's speeches!

It was a powerful, memorable radio broadcast, and it led to a friendship that lasted until Cy's death. He not only recited the words, he walked the talk. He lived Dr. King's message. Our relationship led to multiple multi-racial experiences in my life. I loved the man!

Cy Young made an incredible impact on this young broadcaster and musician.

Maurice Henry Carter

I first met Maurice in the mid-1990s, an indigent African American from Gary, Indiana, serving a life sentence in the State of Michigan for something he said he didn't do. I worked side-by-side with him for the next decade to free him and to prove that the state was wrong. During that time we became brothers, and my family became his family.

To my dismay, we never cleared his name. Over the years a large team was amassed to help Maurice, but the best we could do was obtain a compassionate release for him in 2003 because he was suffering in the late stages of Hepatitis C. He died three months after he walked out of prison.

In Black History Month, 2015, I would be remiss if I did not pay tribute to these three wonderful people of color. I thank God that, in his plan for my life, he arranged these amazing acquaintances! Now my life is filled with people of varied racial and ethnic backgrounds. How rich I am!

Turning a frown into a smile
Sunday, January 25, 2015

I remembered her face and her frown.

This prisoner wasn't touched by any of our songs or any of our words when HFP's musical group SWEET FREEDOM presented a gospel concert at the Michigan prison for women. I was playing keyboard, facing the audience, so my eyes kept getting drawn to this one person who obviously wasn't having a good time. Perhaps she had come with a friend, just as a favor. She remained for the entire program but she didn't seem to like it.

That was last June, and I had completely forgotten about her until yesterday.

Board Chairman Dan Rooks and I were in the same auditorium in the same prison, as guest speakers for a public assembly sponsored by the local chapter of the National Lifers Association. I spoke first.

I so enjoy meeting with the women at this prison, because it's a love affair, in the honorable sense of the word. HUMANITY FOR PRISONERS loves and works hard for these women, and they are most grateful for our compassion and assistance.

The same girl, with the same frown, was in the very same seat. As I discussed our successes and our failures, our services and our goals, it was just like the concert. Nothing phased her.

Then it was Dan's turn. A clinical psychologist, Dan's presentation style is in stark contrast to my effervescence. I'm sure it resembles his quiet, confident manner in a personal counseling session. He chose the life and the problems of a patient as his primary example. The parallels became obvious in a hurry. The woman had made bad decision after bad decision, and by the time she came to Dan her life was a disaster, and so was her self-esteem.

As he calmly explained what negative feelings and actions had to be abandoned, what positive feelings and actions can do to turn a life around and restore self-esteem, the girl with the frown sat up and took notice. As he discussed handling feelings in time of grief and anger, quoting from excellent resource material, Miss Frowning Face leaned forward, obviously eager to catch the next word.

Dan's message was one of hope. His example of the disciple who betrayed Jesus seemed to resonate. Jesus was not only Peter's Lord, but his best friend, and yet in a sad moment, he made a bad decision. But when his eyes connected with Jesus following the three incidents, Peter saw not only hurt, but love and compassion. This powerful servant of our Lord was not only forgiven, but went on to become the founder of the Christian church.

The young woman was now swiping tears from her cheeks.

In the Q&A session that followed, her hand was the first up, admitting that she was moved by Dan's presentation and asking if copies of his resource material, especially dealing with grief, were available. And her opinion about me and HFP had also taken a turn: "How can my family support your organization," she asked.

My simple point: God didn't use our fine gospel music or my up-beat HFP presentation to touch a life. He used Dr. Dan to hold up a mirror, and let this troubled young woman see her own reflection.

It was just one highlight of a beautiful session with beautiful friends.

Think we could release half of them?
Monday, January 12, 2015

Bryan Stevenson makes an amazing claim! He says that a million people in our jails and prisons are in for non-violent crimes and could be released today! He didn't develop the point in his lecture in the Calvin January Series, but the implications were clear: the release would not make a negative impact on society, and it would save us a ton of money.

He said this after pointing out that the United States makes up 5% of the world's population, but shamefully claims 25% of the world's incarcerated individuals. We have 2.2 million people behind bars!

That statement started my thought processes. Right here in Michigan, where we have more than 40,000 people in our state prison system alone, Matt and I see numerous categories of prisoners who could and should be released.

I'll not go into a lot of detail, but here are some that we believe could be let out today:

PAROLABLE LIFERS NOW ELIGIBLE FOR PAROLE
The Parole Board just keeps hanging onto a bunch of these people for no apparent reason. They're eligible for parole, they're not causing problems, and they're getting older.

SENIOR CITIZENS
We have a geriatric division in Coldwater not unlike your neighborhood nursing home. Old folks in beds and wheelchairs, demanding intensive care and posing a threat to no one. The cost to care for these inmates is exceptionally high.

ALCOHOLICS/DRUG ADDICTS
True, they need help. Prison isn't the right place.

MENTALLY ILL

Ditto. 25-50% of Michigan prisoners are mentally challenged. Our prisons have taken the place of psychiatric hospitals.

THOSE CONVICTED OF DRUG OFFENSES
In our effort to be tough on crime, we have imposed exceptionally stiff sentences on persons arrested for minor drug violations. In many cases, the kingpins never got arrested.

SERIOUSLY ILL, TERMINALLY ILL AND SERIOUSLY HANDICAPPED
Stop to think about it. These people are not going to re-offend. In many situations it is inhumane to deny family care. And, in our opinion, it is NOT being insensitive to victims to show compassion here.

We don't have accurate statistics reflecting just how many prisoners we're talking about, and we can't prove that it amounts to 50% of the Michigan prison population.

It doesn't take an expert, however, to conclude that prison is not the proper environment for many people in these categories. Our prison population would be dramatically reduced!

The challenge is to get our elected officials on the same page.

That's up to you and me.

Michigan's shameful treatment of mentally ill inmates
Sunday, December 28, 2014

It doesn't take long to figure out what's wrong with Michigan prisoner Mr. T.

You don't have to spend hours trying to decipher the awkward hand-writing in a meandering 5-page letter, or the stack of poorly prepared grievances, or the attached medical and psychological reports.

Here's what you'll find:

- **two suicide attempts**

- **personal attacks by inmates**

- **verbal abuse by guards**

- **various medical issues, some serious, some treated, some not**

- **misconduct tickets, often for "insolence."**

Mr. T. is mentally ill.

This subject keeps rearing its ugly head as Matt and I try to address the problems of inmates. A good share of our prisoners are mentally challenged, staff-members aren't properly trained to handle them, and many fellow-prisoners don't know how to deal with them. As a result, tragic stories, hundreds of them very much like this...and nothing happening!

Reading between the lines, it's easy to see how staff members say unkind things to this man, how doctors finally give up on trying to deal with his aches and pains, how the psychologist struggles with medication issues, how fellow-inmates treat him poorly, and ultimately how he feels alone and abandoned. And, it would be easy to laugh

127

this off as many staff members do, joking that it's just another deranged person ranting and raving.

But, here's the problem: Mr. T. is a child of God. He's also a son, possibly a brother, possibly a father, possibly an uncle. Jesus loves him. Through no fault of his own, he got sent to the wrong institution for care. He's now a ward of the state, and that means our tax dollars are being spent, or misspent.

Another inmate complained this week that things are crawling around beneath her skin. Different symptoms, same problem. She thinks no one cares. She insists no one is helping her. She's mentally ill.

And the Parole Board, also an arm of the MDOC, isn't helping matters. In a recent interview, a mentally challenged inmate was told that she couldn't be considered for release to a psychiatric hospital until she started behaving! Duh!

The state admits that about 25% of its prisoners have mental issues. We think it's closer to 50%! Either way, it's past time to do something about it. You must talk to your state legislators. Go the Governor. Go to the Director of the Department of Corrections. Your church should protest. Mental health advocates should be up in arms. It's going to take a lot of pushing and shoving. We're going to have to cause a lot of commotion. But there's no alternative.

Michigan prisons are not mental institutions, which means that 25-50% of their occupants are not being cared for properly. And their problems are not simple issues that HFP can help solve. These people deserve real help. Now!

What are you going to do about it?

Human Rights Day: Phhtttt!
Wednesday, December 10, 2014

Isn't it ironic that today, December 10, is Human Rights Day?

Human Rights Day is a global observance, not a national holiday, and nothing that will give kids a day off, close banks or stop your daily mail. It was developed by the UN way back in the 1940s, following the Second World War.

Its observance is marred today.

ON THE NATIONAL LEVEL, The United States has been disgraced by newly released reports showing that our country used torture on detainees who, it was believed, may have been involved with or had contact with those who brought about the 9/11 attack in New York. It's a shameful day in U.S. history.

But torture isn't limited to just the national and international arenas.

ON THE STATE LEVEL, our office is dealing with a first-hand report from inside the women's prison located in Ypsilanti regarding a mentally ill inmate: *The last 18 months she has been locked in an Observation Cell without showering, reading material, or any form of human contact, for mail is not allowed. Now she is locked in a room without a mattress, for they say she tore off a string. The food the mentally ill are served is a joke: peanut butter/jelly sandwiches, cookies, sliced bananas, graham crackers, for EVERY MEAL for a year! That's cruel and unusual punishment.*

And just this week we received a report

ON THE LOCAL LEVEL: *Three local police officers show up at a downstate woman's home in the evening while her children were there. They tell her*

129

she's under arrest because she has not gotten her blinker repaired in the time frame her fix-it ticket specified. (She gets paid every two weeks and was waiting for a paycheck.) The amount needed was $285. Her parents wired the money via Western Union and it arrived at 9:30 p.m. She was not released until 1:30 a.m.

The mother tells me she called the police department to make sure her daughter was there and a male officer said, "Oh, the fat lady?" The mother told the officer her daughter was diabetic and had a heart condition and asked if her daughter had her meds with her. They said not. The mother said, "You can't do that to her." The officer said, "We can do anything we want."

In jail the woman was put in a holding cell with other men and women, some bloodied from domestic and other violence. She asked for something to eat. The officer told her, "You look like you should lose some weight." She never received anything to eat — or meds.

It's past time to sit in our easy chairs and cluck our teeth over alleged human rights violations. It's past time to say things like that only happen in other places. On Human Rights Day, 2014, let's get off our duffs and say, "No more!" Support your favorite organization that deals with these issues, and express your immediate displeasure with any and all of your elected public officials who don't represent what you feel and believe. Your dollars and your voices count!

130

It's your turn to speak
Sunday, November 2, 2014

So here's the deal.

If you agree that if kids are too young to drink, too young to smoke, too young to drive, they should also be too young to receive life sentences or to serve time with hardened criminals in adult prisons;

If you agree that it's time for Michigan to release many of its older, medically fragile and incapacitated prisoners;

If you agree that successor judges should not have veto-power over Parole Board decisions;

If you agree that the Michigan Parole Board is taking over the sentencing role of judges in many cases, especially those involving CSC convictions;

If you agree that Michigan sentencing guidelines should be revised to better ensure that similar offenders who commit similar offenses receive similar sentences;

If you agree with national and state research that shows that simply keeping people in prison longer does not keep the public safer;

If you agree that it's time to change Michigan's reputation of keeping people behind bars longer than most other states;

If you agree, after reading this list, that sentencing reform and Parole Board reform must happen in the State of Michigan;

Then you gotta go to the polls! Pure and simple.

Every time I make a presentation I find people in the audience who are vocal about state government and the

Michigan Department of Corrections, but then admit that they don't know the names of their State Representatives and State Senators. They'll express themselves with a loud voice in a public meeting, but have never given their opinion to a state legislator.

Your vote can and will make a difference. Together we can bring about change. Your chance comes on Tuesday.

If you're not going to vote, don't even bother to speak up on all these issues. Your actions are so loud your words cannot be heard!

On feelings of remorse
Thursday, October 16, 2014

Originally posted on January 7, 2012

A friend of HFP sent in a copy of an editorial that I had written three years ago. It deserves a reprint.

"We hear this all the time!" Assistant Michigan Attorney General Thomas Kulick, with a smirk on his face, in the spotlight at a public hearing this week. "Prisoners are always trying to convince us that they are feeling remorse."

Kulick was responding to the whispered words of a dying inmate, cringing in a wheelchair before him, seeking permission to spend his final days outside of prison . The inmate merely had stated that he was sorry about his earlier life, and he wished he could do it all over again.

Do you know why you hear those words all the time, Mr. Kulick? It's because the Parole Board from your own state makes that demand!

I speak from experience. If prisoners, especially those accused of a sex offense, ever hope to get a parole, they must confess to the crime, and they must show remorse. <u>This comes from the mouths of Parole Board members.</u>

And so, Mr. Kulick, you should be able to predict the results, but I'll explain them anyway.

1. People, falsely accused, sometimes violate all the principles they have been taught, and tell lies to the Parole Board, just because they cannot stand the prison environment anymore and will do anything to get out.

2. Meanwhile, the "con artists" in prison, persons who should not be out on the street, know how to work the system. They weep, they grovel, they say all the words the Parole Board members want to hear. They know what they must do to catch a parole.

3. Yet many people with integrity refuse to compromise. I can still hear the words of the late Maurice Carter, weeks before he died, sitting on a hospital gurney after he was told by former Parole Board Chair John Rubitschun that he could walk free right then if he would merely confess to the crime. He stared at Mr. Rubitschun through his ill-fitting prison-issue glasses, with all the dignity he could muster: *I will never admit to a crime that I did not commit*! He was in prison 29 years.

So do you see how the system works in reverse, Mr. Kulick?

The prisoners who should remain behind bars find a way to wreak havoc once again in society, while those who maintain their honor are punished by receiving a flop: that is, they are refused parole for another period of time. Sadly, they remain behind bars.

It's no surprise that you hear words of remorse, Mr. Kulick. That's what is expected.

Now it's about time that the citizens of Michigan hear words of remorse from you, your office and the Michigan Parole Board, for missing the whole point!

Water torture is real
Tuesday, September 9, 2014

We'd like to shed a little more light on the subject of water, and how it is sometimes used to torment and abuse mentally challenged Michigan prisoners...and not just women.

I hope you read the MLive story, written by a reporter for the Ann Arbor News, outlining alleged abuse of two female inmates at the women's prison in Ypsilanti. One of the claims was water deprivation.

First you should know what the American Bar Association has to say about food and water deprivation: **Correctional authorities should not withhold food or water from any prisoner.**

I guess the staff at the women's prison doesn't feel these guidelines apply, because here's what the mother of one of those inmates told me today: "Chief Christine Wilson (head of the acute unit) said they can keep food away for 24 hours and water for 3 or 4 days. She said that they can do that when a person is in segregation." 3 or 4 days?!

But stuff like this has been going on for years.

Some ten years ago my friend Mary Ann reported that her mentally challenged brother was placed in segregation on a hot summer day by prison guards. And then, just to enhance the punishment, they turned off the cold water. All he had in his cell was hot water.

Shutting off water in a prisoner's cell falls within state policy, but the policy goes on to say that inmates must be given water from time to time. Lois DeMott, mother of a young man who had been struggling with mental issues while in prison, says, "The problem is, water is not provided then according to policy." She cites stories about her son as proof.

135

Who can forget the tragic account of Timmy Souders who died, chained to the prison floor, on a sweltering summer day in a Michigan prison? That was back in 2007. The feature on 60 Minutes can still be seen on-line.

DeMott, now coordinator of the Family Participation Program for Michigan prisons, flatly states that these detestable practices continue to occur in all segregation units in Michigan facilities. She contends that it is "normal practice" by some officers who, she says, "think their walls are so high they can get away with it." And one of the reasons is that, so far, they have gotten away with it.

That's precisely why we fed the ACLU these shocking details from Ypsilanti, and that's precisely why the letter was written. It was time for us to stand up and be counted.

ACLU attorneys will be meeting with the Director of the MDOC on the 15th.

Think we'll see any change?

One person CAN make a difference!
Thursday, August 28, 2014

It wasn't that Ms. S wanted to get even. She just wanted to be able to sleep at night.

Ms. S had a prison job as a volunteer. She was assigned to be an observer in a unit where mentally ill prisoners are housed. Some may be suicidal, and the state wants to catch the problem before it worsens. The Michigan Department of Corrections says that this program has been quite successful.

But in the case of Ms. S, she claims that she witnessed atrocities that should not have happened. A woman of faith, she takes her Christianity seriously and felt that she could no longer remain silent when mentally ill prisoners were being abused. Besides that, those visions of evil-doing kept her awake at night.

And so she spoke out, not only in the prison system, but to sources outside the prison. Retaliation was predictable and swift. She lost her coveted job as a volunteer. Her communications were monitored. Prison life became difficult. But Ms. S was not to be deterred.

She had witnessed shameful treatment of two mentally ill inmates, and daily she fed her information to outside contacts. One woman was actually hogtied, and left that way "until she could learn to behave." Another was denied a sip of water until she was so dehydrated she could no longer drink. The second victim was given drugs to sedate her, but even after she was unconscious a nurse continued the injections. Eventually the inmate was rushed to the hospital by ambulance. Life support has now been removed, and word is that she will not survive.

Ms. S not only detailed these atrocities in daily dispatches, but persuaded other volunteers to sign on. We have in our possession clumsy affidavits on bits and pieces of paper signed by additional courageous volunteers who dared to stand up and be counted.

For weeks nothing happened, as the HFP office continued to stir the pot behind the scenes. But then came some movement. The ACLU, with co-signers from the U of M Law School, sent a scathing 5-page letter to the director of the MDOC as well as the prison warden demanding changes and requesting an immediate meeting. Ammunition for this letter was provided by HFP. In addition, our office filed a complaint with the U.S. Department of Justice regarding these alleged 8th Amendment violations: cruel and unusual punishment. This week, according to inside sources, the DOJ was to make an appearance at the prison in Ypsilanti. As a third step, HFP consulted with legal counsel in hopes of initiating legal action on behalf of a victim's family.

If the state will not listen to the voices of the little people, perhaps it will take note of the collective voices of the DOJ, the ACLU and the U of M. Perhaps the threat of legal action will get some attention.

There will be changes in the way mentally ill women are treated in prison. You can bet on it.

We can all learn an important lesson from this. Silence is not an option when we witness wrong-doing. One person can make a difference.

Perhaps, in between psych-therapy sessions, our whistle blower, Ms. S, would have time to take a bow.

She deserves it.

Same old, same old
Friday, July 25, 2014

This was an amazing weekend exactly 10 years ago. Maurice Carter was free, after serving 29 years for a crime he did not commit. It was a time of celebration and elation!

Today, one decade later, Matt and I sit in the office that fulfills the Carter dream. And as we sit here, I'm wondering just how much progress has been made in the way Michigan handles prisoners.

Maurice was granted a compassionate release...he was not exonerated. He was in the final stages of Hepatitis C, and he desperately needed a liver transplant. He had been diagnosed with Hep-C 8 years earlier, but the state just didn't bother to share that information with him. Things haven't changed much.

It took the Governor one full year to grant the release, even though Maurice was dying and could not survive without a transplant. Things haven't changed much.

Before even granting the public hearing, the chairman of the Parole Board at that time offered Maurice an immediate release if he would simply confess to the crime for which he had been charged. Things haven't changed much.

In the public hearing, an assistant from the Michigan Attorney General's office strongly and loudly protested Maurice Carter's release. To that sadly misguided individual, Maurice was still a serious threat to society. Things haven't changed much.

This marked the first time in his 29 years that Maurice even managed to get in front of the Parole Board. Even though he had been eligible for parole for a long time, every time his name came up for a PB review the board simply sent a form letter expressing "no interest." Things haven't changed much.

We keep hearing demands about prison reform in Michigan, and God knows we need it. But we hear very few demands for change with the Michigan Parole Board. This little group of 10 people has an incredible grip over thousands and thousands of lives, and thousands and thousands of tax dollars. Every time the board rejects parole for one eligible lifer, for example, that inmate must remain behind bars for another 5 years, and the cost to the state is almost a quarter of a million dollars!

We keep people in prison longer than any other state, ladies and gentlemen, and it's costing us a fortune! It's time to take a close, hard look at the Michigan Parole Board.

It's time to demand change and improvement!

Michigan's forgotten prisoners
Sunday, July 6, 2014

The Lord himself...will never leave you or forsake you...do not be discouraged.

I'm sure that these words from Moses to Joshua, as quoted in Deuteronomy 31, have been a comfort to millions of people over the years.

They came to my mind over the weekend as HFP deals with a little-known problem in the Michigan prison system: the plight of prisoners with long, indeterminate sentences.

The situation is this: Some insensitive judges, perhaps hoping to make a statement, handed down sentences far worse than life in prison. Here are two examples. My friend Troy Chapman, instead of receiving a parolable life sentence, was given 60 to 90 years. Another prisoner whom I don't know, but whose situation was revealed in an AP story this weekend, is Leon Echols. His sentence was 75 to 150 years!

And here's the problem. Thanks to an opinion by the Michigan Attorney General in 1986, these guys are not eligible for parole until they serve their minimum. This means that Chapman, who is 50 and who has already served 29 years; and Echols, who is 43 and has served nearly 25 years, will both be in their 80s by the time they get to meet with the Parole Board. Lifers, on the other hand, after serving x number of years in prison, get a crack at the Parole Board every 5 years.

Both of these inmates have tried unsuccessfully to get their sentences commuted by the Governor, which he certainly could do. But why should he? A commutation would do little to reduce Michigan's shamefully high prison population, and on the other hand it definitely could damage his political reputation. Being tough on crime pleases voters.

141

We don't know how many of these prisoners with long, indeterminate sentences are buried and forgotten in Michigan prisons, but you can be sure that Troy and Leon aren't the only two!

Perhaps AP Writer Ed White's story, published in various Michigan newspapers this weekend, is a start. But we mustn't stop there. Corrective legislation is needed. HFP is going to do its part. You can do yours, as well. Simply passing this piece along to someone of influence might make a difference.

We know the Lord won't leave these guys or forsake them.

Will we?

Whistle blowers behind bars: Heroes!
Thursday, June 26, 2014

Thanks to behind-the-bars whistle blowers, HFP is providing an exceptional service. But I'm not sure it's having the desired effect.

We are so proud of those inmates who leak the truth to us on a regular basis by email and letter. We have learned which ones are exaggerating, are telling self-serving stories, and are determined to smear the system. We have reputable people behind bars who are regularly disclosing serious problems in Michigan prisons, and we are sharing that information.

In recent months we have told about a mentally ill woman being hog-tied in the nude for hours, and being forced to sleep on a slab with no padding.

We are now receiving reports of another mentally ill woman who was denied food and water, and who was administered drugs even while still unconscious from the previous injection. Only then was she rushed to a hospital by ambulance on a ventilator.

From Michigan's Woodland Facility, which houses mentally ill men, come new reports of abuse and lack of appropriate care, and then cover-up moves by staff members.

The daily messages on the HFP network are not there to titillate the reader.

We don't put them out there to replicate the super-sensational tabloids.

We do this to inform an uninformed public. But more than that, we also expect results.

In almost every session where I make a presentation, people ask what they can do about these intolerable situations. Certainly we can pray for improvement, but we must do more than that. We must demand change.

If nothing else, as a state tax payer, here's why you should care. Michigan prisons take a bigger bite out of the general fund budget than any other state. Michigan keeps people in prison longer than any other state. You and I are paying for it!

And there are problems in the Michigan prisons which we are revealing daily on our email network, thanks to whistle blowers who know that they can expect retaliation. Much of it we also share in our monthly newsletter.

Do you know the name of your State Representative? How about your State Senator? Have you ever contacted either of them? They are not appointed...they are elected to office. If you're a registered voter in the state, they'll listen to you. And if they don't, you should vote for someone else and you should tell them that.

Sign up for our email network. Sign up to receive our monthly newsletter. Then, when you get this disturbing information, dare to do something about it!

For those of us who consider ourselves Christians and responsible American citizens, we have no option.

Complacency is a sin.

A way to remember Andrew
Wednesday, June 11, 2014

Almost mid-month, and HFP contributions coming in slowly.

Then, a heart-breaking letter arrived yesterday. Here is the message, in part:

Dear Mr. Tjapkes:

A few months ago I wrote to you regarding my son Andrew, and the difficult time he was having at Pugsley receiving medical attention. Today is his birthday. My son had back problems and suffered from depression. I have wanted to write to you many times, but was unable to do so because it was too painful. My son took his own life on January 30 of this year. I am inconsolable. Those are the only words I know when someone asks me how I am. I am raising my grandson, who will now never have a relationship with his father. My son was 28 years old and spent the last 10 years struggling with so many demons, and trying so hard to hold on. I ask myself over and over "what will I do without him? What will I do without him?" I am destroyed daily thinking about his last moments and that I could not be with him.

There is no one to be angry with because there are so many to be angry with. The system that failed him for so many years. The way we run our mental health and drug rehab in this country. My son's inability to reach out for real help. Our justice and prison system which is so seriously flawed that prison is somewhere where we just throw our citizens away instead of rehabilitating them, taking away their basic human rights. The fact that unless you have money in this country you are basically just thrown to the wolves.

The day my son died a man from the prison called me, and he didn't even get my son's first name right. Then they literally threw all of his belongings in a box, taped it up and sent it to me—loose salt shakers spilling all over photographs. I called the deputy warden and told him they should be ashamed of themselves to do this to me. I told him that Andrew was someone's child, and they had no right to disrespect him or me in this way.

Every day I receive the emails from you with news from the prisons and prayers, and I read every one. But I am so angry and feel so powerless that with each one I tell myself I will unsubscribe because I can't take anymore of the pain and humiliation these people are being subjected to. I pray every day and I ask for guidance. I ask for strength. I am writing this letter because I know you are someone who understands, and who fights so hard for prisoners rights. I have no money, sir. But I know that I need to do something to help change things. I need to do something in my son's name, to change anything that I can. But I don't know what to do.

I thank you for the advice you tried to give us. I thank you for what you do each day to help people who can't help themselves. I have no more words. God Bless,

Kim

Well, I know what to do, Kim. It won't bring Andrew back, but it will help us to assist more mothers and more sons facing similar problems. We'll invite HFP supporters to make a one-time donation in memory of Andrew to keep this ministry alive. It founders every month, almost never meeting budget.

In June, 2014, perhaps we can hit our goal, in the name of your son.

146

Matt will post a separate figure each day showing Andrew Memorial Contributions.

May God be near this hurting mother, and all the other prison moms.

Treating prisoners worse than animals
Sunday, May 4, 2014

Matt and I got a dose of reality last week.

We had been invited to an in-service training session by a local attorney who likes and supports the work of HUMANITY FOR PRISONERS.

He had recently won settlements in two cases of cruel and unusual punishment of mentally ill inmates, and he wanted to give us pointers as to when there might be violations of the 8th Amendment. But here was the shocker: He informed us that treating prisoners like animals is not bad enough...the courts won't look at those cases. The only time there is grounds for a civil suit, he said, is when the prison system treats an inmate **worse than an animal**. Only then is it time to consider action.

He gave an example of a mentally ill prisoner who injured his finger behind bars, and it didn't get treated properly. It got infected, he was taken to the hospital, and the finger was amputated. Not cruel and unusual punishment, said the lawyer. But when the inmate was returned to jail, he was refused his pain medication. And while suffering excruciating pain and banging on his door to get his meds, he was maced by the guard. That was the tipping point. Refusing pain medication and shooting gas into the face of the inmate for trying to get attention was a violation of the 8th amendment. The lawyer sued on behalf of the inmate and his family, and won.

This means that many of the complaints we receive do not meet the criteria of cruel and unusual punishment. True, there are many areas where one might complain of medical malpractice, and there are often cases where corrections officers behave in an unprofessional manner, but the courts ain't gonna take a look at that. It's gotta be worse!

148

Right now we're looking at a claim that a mentally ill inmate was not only hog-tied as punishment, but was forced to sleep on a steel slate for a week with no mattress. If those claims are true, we're going for the jugular. Not acceptable. That is treating a prisoner worse than an animal.

HFP is watching, and poised.

A sad, short story...may it make you sick!
Wednesday, April 9, 2014

I never cease to be amazed as to how human beings treat human beings.

It was a simple telephone call to the HFP office. Could we help a guy just released from the federal prison system? The situation was desperate.

The short answer was no. There are agencies that handle things like this. We don't. HFP works as an advocacy agency for persons IN prison, and only in the state prison system.

But then the lady from this re-entry agency went on to tell her story.

The man was injured while he was in the federal prison system. She informed me in a calm and matter-of-fact manner that the injuries left the man a paraplegic. No surprise. No emotion. Just the facts, ma'am. He entered as a healthy man...he departed as a cripple.

John Doe became eligible for release...and was then released to what was called a half-way house in the Detroit area. He went there because he had no family, no friends, nobody to care for him. A paraplegic. Alone. The kind of person Jesus talked about.

But, things didn't go well at this place. You see, there are rules you must abide by. Rules are important...for prisoners, and for the released. And one of these rules involved cell phones.

The man was simply trying to get some treatment for his health issues, being a paraplegic and all...but he used the cell phone when he wasn't supposed to. Only certain hours for cell phones. Sorry. So he was evicted!

Never mind that he can't get around, that he has no one, that there is no other program to take him in. He's out!

God bless America!

Somebody's gonna be held accountable for this kinda crap someday!

Lent: A season to reflect on our treatment of prisoners
Friday, March 7, 2014

The season of Lent is certainly the most meaningful of all seasons in the Christian year.

I hate what they did to Jesus.

I love what he did for me.

How barbaric the people were back in Bible times! The guards teased and taunted and abused Jesus. He suffered through a brief kangaroo court session. He was sentenced to death in a wrongful conviction. And the method of execution was especially designed to punish the condemned with more than just death. Crucifixion was just plain cruel.

Times have certainly changed, right?

No more ridicule and abuse by guards. No more kangaroo court sessions. No more wrongful convictions.

True, we don't have crucifixions in this country. We don't even have hangings or firing squads.

But until 1999 we were still using gas chambers. In 1983 the State of Mississippi decided to clear people out of the viewing room when a gasping prisoner refused to die after 8 minutes of torture in the chamber.

The electric chair, no longer being used, is still being romanticized. "Old Sparky," it was called in many states. Texas has Old Sparky on display in its prison museum in Huntsville, right near the spot where the state continues to punish people with execution. As viewers watched in horror, the hair of an inmate being electrocuted actually caught on fire.

Now we use a more "civilized" means of taking the lives of prisoners...the lethal injection. I personally viewed one of those killings, and refuse to call it civilized.

Perhaps the season of Lent would be the perfect time to listen once again to the teachings of the risen Savior.

As I recall, he said the way we treat prisoners is actually to be considered the way we treat him.

Heroes behind bars? You bet!
Sunday, March 2, 2014

The whole concept of heroes sometimes bothers me.

The people who are referred to as heroes in the media today often aren't my heroes.

When I was an active newsman, I liked to pay tribute to the most unlikely of heroes: the caregivers in nursing homes, the cops and firemen, ambulance personnel, school bus drivers.

Today, in my third and final career, I see many real heroes. And they're in prison.

Let me list a few:

The guy who decides to run interference for a dying inmate who is being harassed by guards because of the large hernia lump in his abdomen

The guy who agrees to let a handicapped inmate who must walk in a crouching position cling to his belt, despite the teasing and taunting from staff

The guys who keep their faith, even though being wrongly convicted on sex charges due to false testimony by ex-wives, former girlfriends, and naughty school kids

The guy who should have been released by the Parole Board long ago, but instead of pouting leads a daily Bible study

The guy who knows he's in prison for a reason, but dares to say that his co-defendant was railroaded and is not guilty

The girl who begs for someone to befriend a senior citizen who the courts claim was responsible for the death of a grandchild, because she now feels alone and abandoned behind bars

The girl who chooses to make a monthly donation to HFP, even though she earns less than 90 cents a day

The girl who refuses to waste her time moping, and leads a committee in the National Lifers Association to seek legislation for judicial reform

The guy who listens to the stories of inmates returning from public hearings, and publishes a guideline for others to better prepare for these hearings

The guys and the girls who are concerned about the attitudes of young inmates just arriving, and use their spare time for mentoring

And this is the tip of the iceberg. Matt and I encounter these heroes every day.

An HFP salute to these unsung heroes. May God continue to bless them and raise up more.

Holidays without a loved one
Thursday, December 19, 2013

The joy of the holiday season is tarnished for those who lost someone dear to them in the past year.

For those of us working with prisoners and the prison system, we know there will be stories involving deaths of loved ones...but HFP is going to try to make a difference in the new year!

Our resolution to try to bring about change was strengthened last week when I spoke to James.

We lost another prisoner this past week, man...another one of our guys passed. He had lung cancer. He had been coughing and choking. We knew he was in bad shape. The docs had recommended a compassionate release to the Parole Board last year and it was turned down. The Parole Board considered another request this year and turned it down. That's so sad. It didn't have to be that way, man. He had family that just wanted him home for his last days.

That's the kind of stuff that just about sends me to the moon.

Who are these people who decide that a dying inmate, regardless of how serious the crime that sent him there, is still a threat to society? In our discussion, James then told me of another inmate who died of liver cancer shortly before that.

HUMANITY FOR PRISONERS was saddened in 2013 when we lost Joey and Otto. We heard of Linda's death in the women's infirmary. These prisoners could have and should have been home, surrounded by friends and loved ones. Instead, they died alone in a cold, impersonal atmosphere. What a shame!

If the past holds true, some 125 prisoners will die in the Michigan prison system in 2014, and about 60% of those will be from natural causes.

The HFP Board of Directors has determined that we must make a strong push for two things in 2014: getting Hospice care into the prison system for those who are dying; and doing our best to increase the number of compassionate releases for those inmates who are terminally ill.

Obviously, the state has no heart.

We're about to demonstrate again that HFP does.

Mandela and Carter: heroes, models
Friday, December 6, 2013

The world is grieving the loss of one of its brightest shining stars today. A script-writer could not have improved on the story of Nelson Mandela, incarcerated for a third of his life and then ascending to the presidency of his country.

As I listen to the various commentators the morning after, I am reminded time and again of my personal experience with a man, also of dark skin, who spent half of his life in prison for a crime he did not commit.

I hear statements that tell how Mr. Mandela touched lives around the world.

And I hear questions like: How could a man in prison for 27 years come out without being bitter?

I've been blessed to meet two men who had similar experiences. Both were named Carter. And as in the Mandela case, racism was involved.

Rubin Hurricane Carter, wrongly convicted not just once, but twice, told me that one day he looked in an old, cracked mirror in the prison and saw the reflection of a man he didn't even know. It was the portrait of a bitter and angry individual. He said that he made the decision right then to change, because "if I remained angry," he said, "they would be the winner, and I couldn't allow that to happen." Dr. Carter turned out to be one of the most warm and charming individuals I have ever met. He, too, touched lives around the world.

Maurice Henry Carter was something else. This indigent black man from Gary, Indiana, was arrested and imprisoned here in Michigan for a crime he didn't commit, and he was not a model prisoner for the first period of his incarceration. Would you be?

158

But he also told me that midway through his time in prison he made the decision to bury hatred, and try to turn his wrongful conviction into something positive. Unbeknownst to me, God used even me to help him change his attitude. When I joined his fight for freedom, nine years before his release, he realized that there could be people who care and that God had not abandoned him.

Maurice was in prison for 29 years...two years longer than Nelson Mandela. He didn't have the name recognition of a world leader, but I'm proud to say that before he died in 2004 he, too, touched lives—many, many of them—all around the world!

The sad thing is that we don't seem to listen to people like Mandela, Carter and Carter...and we don't seem to learn from them.

South Africa may be making progress, but here in this country, leadership by our first African American president has driven a segment of our population into a frenzy. And our government is taking steps backward to once again make it more difficult for people of color to vote. We also imprison an amazingly imbalanced number of young African American men.

I hear, through Mandela and Carter and Carter, these words of Jesus: **Love your enemies and pray for those who persecute you.**

We still have a lot to learn.

Think of prisoners when lighting the HOPE candle
Sunday, December 1, 2013

I love the season of Advent...a time of expectation and anticipation. Dennis Bratcher, of the Christian Resources Institute, in explaining the meaning of this season, said: **There is a yearning for deliverance from the evils of the world, first expressed by Israelite slaves in Egypt as they cried out from their bitter oppression. It is the cry of those who have experienced the tyranny of injustice...**

And that made me think of Advent, 2013, where we still have hundreds of thousands of people behind bars, who right now cry out from their bitter oppression. Many are experiencing the tyranny of injustice. Some have been wrongly convicted, many have been over-charged and/or over-sentenced. Many are experiencing cruel treatment. Many are suffering the torture of solitary confinement. These aren't just empty words of speculation...these are words of truth right from the office of HUMANITY FOR PRISONERS.

At the beginning of each week of Advent, many Christians light a candle on the Advent Wreath. And today's the day for the first candle: the candle of Hope.

The words of Dennis Bratcher again: **It is that hope, however faint at times, and that God, however distant he sometimes seems, which brings to the world the anticipation of a king who will rule with truth and justice...It is that hope that once anticipated, and now anticipates anew, the reign of an Anointed One, a Messiah, who will bring peace and justice and righteousness to the world...**

160

It seems to me that, on this first Sunday of Advent, until his second coming, it's up to those of us who follow this Messiah, to do everything we can to kindle and enhance that hope among the incarcerated. They must get the message that we care. They must be able to hear our cries for truth and justice. They must witness first-hand our expressions of love and peace...in deeds, not just words.

It's wonderful to anticipate the arrival of him who will finally bring peace and justice and righteousness to our society. But until then, the burden is on those of us who bear his title.

Third world jail? Nope, Michigan prison
Friday, November 15, 2013

I've had it!

We may not treat women this way!

You've been reading and hearing about the toilet and shower shortages during remodeling and repairs in one of the women's prison units. At one point, 74 women with no toilet...inmates forced to go to the unit next door.

Now the HFP office is hearing complaints from women in that unit, who were told to drink less water so they wouldn't have to go to the bathroom as often. These comments came right from a Michigan prison, operated with your tax dollars and mine:

People are dehydrated, with sick stomachs, from not being able to go #2

One girl went to the desk and asked for a bag, she couldn't hold her poo any longer. Officer gave her a paper towel

Some girls had to pee in their trash can

Some officers don't even announce bathroom loud, and if you don't hear it and miss it, too bad...another two hours

They constantly yell at us telling us to hurry up, hurry up...you have 3 minutes to use the bathroom. Under that pressure, who can even go to the bathroom?

Showers, we are told 10 minutes, and that includes getting dressed and undressed. You barely get your body wet and they are yelling at you again:

"Shower's up, get out, turn that water off now, hurry up, Ladies...others are waiting"

We are forced to stuff and stuff and stuff whatever feelings or emotions we may be having. If it gets voiced, we are threatened with a ticket

This could be your mother, your sister, your daughter, your niece.

Make you feel proud to be a Michigander?

A special kind of doctor
Thursday, October 3, 2013

I was in a meeting with officials from the Michigan Department of Corrections, Hospice of Michigan, and Corizon...the health care provider for Michigan prisons. A hospice official asked Mason Gill, VP of Michigan operations for Corizon, about prison doctors. Gill responded that it takes a very special kind of doctor to serve in the prisons.

I'll second that motion.

Let me tell you about a special kind of doctor.

Mr. D. had been complaining about severe pain from a hernia for weeks. Finally, the large lump in his abdomen started turning color and the pain became unbearable. Mr. D. doubled over in pain and started vomiting. He was rushed by ambulance to a local hospital, and then transferred to one of the major hospitals in Lansing. There a surgeon discovered there was not only one, but two hernias...and that the major hernia was causing problems with the colon. He was very upset with the prison healthcare people for letting the situation get to this stage. The surgeon corrected the hernia situation, and then performed a colonoscopy to make sure everything was OK.

Mr. D. was released from the hospital with two provisions. He was given a prescription for pain medication to take him through the post-surgery days. And, he was instructed to come back in two weeks for a post-surgery exam.

Well, let me tell you how that special doctor at the prison reacted.

He was upset that Mr. D. had been sent to the hospital, and said if the decision had been up to him, Mr. D. would have remained in prison.

He refused to fill the prescription for pain meds. Mr. D. would just have to tough it out. After all, he's just a prisoner.

And, he refused to let Mr. D. go back to the surgeon for a post-op exam.

Now that's some special kind of doctor.

How best to tell the story?
Tuesday, September 24, 2013

Son Matt and I will be traveling out of town today. I have been invited to speak at a meeting of one of the popular service clubs...Matt will be there to set up and man the display. We're well aware of what to expect. The make-up of the audience is sure to be all-white, professional and semi-professional people, middle to upper income.

It's early in the morning, and once again as I try to organize my comments, I'm struggling with how to connect with these people. Matt and I have both found that, unless we make a very compelling case, there will be yawns, blank stares, and glances at wrist watches.

These aren't evil people. They're pillars of the community, and certainly many are responsible for major accomplishments in their town. They're nice. They're friendly. But they can't seem to relate.

How do Matt and I make our case? How do we convince them that we're not just a couple of do-gooders showing kindness to people behind bars? We're not trying to set ourselves up as the ones who are REALLY responding to the call of Jesus to care for and visit prisoners. It's up to us to tell what we're experiencing.

There was Doug who was rushed from the prison by ambulance for emergency surgery, who contacted us because he has been denied his post-op pain medication and his post-op doctor's appointment.

There was Dan who was diagnosed years ago with Hepatitis C by prison doctors, but refused treatment. Now he same doctors are telling him the disease is so advanced that his body cannot handle the treatment.

There was Tracy who complained that prison doctors took away her asthma medicine, claiming that she was "faking it."

There was Chris, a paraplegic, who is only being allowed to drain his bladder by catheter once every 12 hours, although standard treatment should be a minimum of 3 times a day...and he's being forced to re-use dirty catheters, which our physician/adviser labels malpractice.

And we've told the stories about the two recent prison deaths in previous blog entries.

How do we convince our audiences that these same people are moms, dads, sisters and brothers, all of whom have the same feelings and emotions that we do? God's children.

May God bless our efforts.

F is for father; F is for forgiveness
Saturday, June 15, 2013

I heard a television commentator discussing fatherhood this week, as he wished all of the fathers in his audience a Happy Father's Day. He said that, as a father, he liked a quote from Henry Ford: *Failure is simply the opportunity to begin again, this time more intelligently.*

FAILURE IS *simply* ·THE· OPPORTUNITY TO { BEGIN } AGAIN THIS TIME MORE INTELLIGENTLY

- Henry Ford

He was right on the money.

I love being a father, but I'm the first to admit that I made a lot of mistakes along the way. I hope that I kept correcting them, when I started over again...with more intelligence. I'm blessed to have a wonderful relationship with my kids and our grandchildren, which means that they all are forgiving people. They don't have a perfect dad or grandpa.

I'm especially mindful of that this year, because in recent days I had to be the message carrier between an elderly prisoner and his adult son. The father is a friend. I do not know the son. Sadly, it didn't turn out well.

The two were reportedly very close at one time, but some demons in the father's life caught up with him and he wound up in prison. Apparently the alleged crime was so heinous that the son absolutely cannot forgive or forget. Now he wants nothing to do with his dad. He ignores messages that come to him from prison. He refuses to do a few little favors that could make life much easier for his father. His focus is only on his hurt feelings and the alleged victims.

When I called the son he said, very openly, "I don't want him anymore. You wanna adopt him?"

He expressed no interest in his father's living conditions or mental state.

And all of this hurt me. In the HFP office we deal with broken relations every day, and I must confess that I have not been in the son's shoes. I loved my dad, and on this day miss him a lot.

But if I claim my heavenly father's promises, that means I am forgiven. No further questions.

I hope on this Father's Day you can forgive your dad, no matter how seriously he messed up. You'd simply be treating him the way you have been treated.

169

Medical un-care
Tuesday, June 4, 2013

Years ago my friend David called me from prison just to chat. He told me that before this telephone call he had been reading to a prisoner. I asked him what that was all about. He explained that the man had recently had eye surgery. because one of his eyes was bad. Problem was the surgery was done on the wrong eye, and now the guy couldn't see. "And they call us the criminals," David said.

For some time I thought that was an isolated incident, but now I'm not so sure. The HFP office is receiving atrocious reports daily.

A woman reported that a friend of hers in Huron Valley had cancer surgery and a very devastating bout of chemo therapy, only to be informed later that she never had cancer. My informant said the state had been getting her friend and another prisoner with the same last name mixed up.

A prisoner reported to me today that personnel in health-care in his facility have been taking away meds from prisoners who have been on that particular regimen for a long period of time. In addition, he said, they're taking away meters from inmates with diabetes. "Somebody's gonna die here," he says.

A wife informed me that her husband has had three surgeries for cancer, but the healthcare people in his particular facility say they don't have the means to give him follow-up treatment, and are unable to take him anywhere for treatment. She's praying for a transfer.

A mother reports that her daughter had the HIV virus when she went into prison, but because the system refused to treat the girl, she now has full-blown AIDS.

Are all these people telling fibs? I don't think so.

The people of the State of Michigan are going to have to demand more from their state legislators, or nothing will get done.

Our nation is opposed to torture, yet I describe this as cruel and unusual punishment. Not in some foreign prison camp. Right here in Pure Michigan.

Big Ben's sermon
Friday, February 22, 2013

My friend Big Ben is a lifer, a dear man who has served some 40 years all because of a foolish moment in his young life. He's a beautiful Christian, and there's really no reason to keep him and many others like him in prison. But that is another matter.

Big Ben informed me the other day that he was recently called on to preach the sermon at the church in prison. He told me about the passage that had chosen.

He went on to tell the congregation about an incident that happened on the floor of the prison gymnasium. He said he was playing a pick-up game of 21 with this guy, and went in for a rebound. When he came down, he slightly brushed his fellow player across the bridge of his nose with an elbow. He said the man went down like a 50-pound sack of potatoes. "I thought he was joking," said Big Ben, "because in my mind I had hardly touched him. But when he lifted his head up, blood was gushing from his nose and his mouth. Naturally I was apologizing profusely, but understandably he didn't want to hear anything of it."

The story didn't end there.

Big Ben didn't see the guy for a few days...but one day he came running up to him, smiling, and hugging him. He was naturally taken aback, and tried to figure out why the change in attitude.

Well as it turns out, the guy's nose had been broken before, and had never healed properly. As a result, he was having a difficult time breathing, and was bothering his bunk-mates with obnoxious snoring. The act of re-breaking his nose actually resulted in the bone re-positioning itself and correcting the man's breathing problem. He was no longer miserable with breathing issues, his snoring stopped, and he was happy.

Big Ben said he concluded the sermon by pointing out that, while he had no conscious part of it, God chose that particular time and place to anoint him with the gift of a healing spirit, and used his body to help relieve the suffering of someone else.

Not bad, Big Ben.

Not bad at all.

All life is precious
Tuesday, February 5, 2013

There's no question that a close brush with death gives a person new appreciation for life. Perhaps that's why the casual way in which life and death are mentioned behind bars makes me so sad.

A friend wrote a short note to me recently from one of Michigan's prisons. Almost as an after-thought, he reported that "there was another murder here last week." Another day, another life.

A female inmate sent a short note via email. "I just thought I would let you know that Trina passed away last night at the hospital. She got pneumonia and her heart gave out. I don't think she had any family."

Another prisoner wrote to tell me of a terrible incident across the hall from him. An inmate jimmied the lock on his cell so the guards couldn't get in...then he tried to beat his roommate to death. They had to just about tear the cell apart to get at him and stop him. I wrote this inmate a short note, asking how the story turned out.

"As for the youngster, the latest word is that he's OK now, out of the hospital. The latest on the guy who tried to kill him is that he committed suicide a couple days ago. Being that he killed a cellie in the past, and now tried to do it again, he knew he was headed back to Level 5, so the word is that's why he hanged himself. I guess he won't be harming anyone else."

Henry Van Dyke said: "Be glad of life, because it gives you the chance to love and to work and to play and to look up at the stars."

Life is cheap behind bars.

We mustn't take it for granted.

175

May God be near the least of these.

Happy new year?
Friday, January 4, 2013

Major issues in Michigan prisons took no holiday vacation.

Minutes after the new year arrived, word of problems also arrived at the HFP office.

From one facility in the UP, one of our good friends was assaulted in a prison bathroom. Later he contacted his family and asked that they try to persuade his warden to place him in protective custody. He was fearing for his life. Happy New Year!

From another facility in the UP came word that violence at that prison continued in full force. An inmate was stabbed in the eye. We are told that when he was rushed to the hospital, they also discovered that he had a broken neck from being stomped on. The story doesn't end there. Word to our office was that by the time guards returned to the man's cell to take care of the victim's property, they discovered that it had all been stolen. Happy New Year!

Speaking of stolen property, an incarcerated pastor reported to us that he and his comrades were locked in the gym of an Ionia prison for four hours during a shake down. That wasn't the major problem. When he returned to his cell, he discovered that his legal work for the past 6 months on a federal appeal was gone. When he complained, guards informed him that he's a prisoner and his property can be searched at any time. Search is one thing, he argued, but theft is another. That's when they transferred him to another prison. Happy New Year!

And those women who are complaining about the heat? Some guy came in the other day to check on the problem, and turned up the fans on the cold air return! No one is certain whether he was just having a bad day or whether this is retaliation for the girls griping about the frigid temperatures. They're hunkering down and adding more layers of clothing. Happy New Year!

FYI, thanks to your support and gifts, we're at the side of all of these people trying to help when and where we can.

Open letter to the boss
Thursday, December 6, 2012

To Mr. Daniel Heyns, Director
MICHIGAN DEPARTMENT OF CORRECTIONS

Dear Mr. Heyns:

You make one generalization in your letter to the editor of the Detroit Free Press, published in the November 11, 2012 edition, that must be challenged. In praising your team of employees, you say this about their work with prisoners: "Every day, they deal with the worst of the worst of Michigan's citizens." It's a generalization that must be challenged. The worst of the worst?

I started going through the HFP files to list exceptions to that rule. I intended to list names of prisoners, and a list of reasons why I so admire these men and women...all of them friends. I found too much material. Many of these inmates have gone 10, 20, 30 and 40 years without one misconduct. They are active in positive programs like the National Lifers Association. They are mentoring and teaching. They are knitting clothing for the underprivileged. They go out of their way to help senior citizens and the mentally ill. They care for the ailing and the injured. Old-timers do their best to give valuable advice to youngsters coming into the system. We encounter it daily. My friend Dr. David Schuringa, President of Crossroad Bible Institute, insists that these are the people that Jesus would enjoy hanging out with. The worst of the worst?

Kenny Wyniemko, wrongly convicted and freed from prison thanks to DNA testing, claims that up to 15% of prisoners may be innocent. Some statistics show that perhaps 20% of Michigan prisoners are mentally ill. The worst of the worst?

How about those employees of yours who do not meet your description of the most dedicated, compassionate, honest and hardest-working? How about those dirty cops who bring in the drugs and allow the resulting illicit activity. How about those guards who tease and abuse the mentally ill, especially the youngsters...the ones who throw a teenager into the hole wearing only his underwear and then open the window on a January day. Or the ones who throw a mentally ill man in the hole on a hot summer day, and turn off his cold water tap. How about the medical people taking away asthma inhaling devices and discontinuing important prescriptions for no particular reason? The medical and dental people refusing basic services?

We hasten to add that we are not to be classified as liberal bleeding hearts who want all prisoners released. We work in the prisons. We know that there are people who belong there. We realize that prisons are here for a reason. We also acknowledge that there are many honest, dedicated, kind people working in the prison system.

Jesus informed his supporters that HE was in prison, chided them for not visiting him, or praised them for calling on him. That wasn't Jesus making the visit. That was Jesus being visited. The worst of the worst?

There are good and bad people behind bars...very much like we have in a free society, and inmates deserve that acknowledgement from the director of our prison system.

Doug Tjapkes, President
HUMANITY FOR PRISONERS

I have a secret
Saturday, September 8, 2012

I get my Bible lessons in the most unusual places. As a church musician, I am often busy practicing at the time of adult Sunday School or Bible study sessions on Sunday morning. But I do not go without Bible study. My good friend and retired pastor Al Hoksbergen and I set aside an hour a week for a little libation and discussion, and this invariably turns into a meaningful lesson for me. This week, I got a bonus. Al and I were asked to do a funeral service. A 90-year-old charter member of our church had died.

I know of no one who does a memorial service better than Al. He doesn't have a "canned sermon" on file for funerals. He not only meets with the families, but then relies on his many years of ministry, preaching, teaching and counseling, to find a perfect match of scripture and the current situation.

The title of the message was "I Have a Secret," and the scripture passage was from Philippians. The Apostle Paul, writing from a prison where he was actually on death row, said "I have learned to be content whatever the circumstances." But he didn't stop there. He said, "I have learned the secret of being content in any and every situation, whether well fed or hungry, whether living in plenty or want."

And that sent my mind in another direction. I didn't listen very well for a few minutes. I was thinking of my prisoner friends. I have a few friends who, like Paul, have learned this secret, and I am astounded every time I hear them speak. I know of two men and a woman who know they don't belong behind bars, know they were treated wrongly, and yet they have the same testimony as St. Paul.

Then I thought about so many others who cannot find that contentment, and it reminded me that we must pray for many, many, many prisoners who are upset, sad, disturbed, angry, and distraught because the system hasn't been fair with them. Those prayers must also be extended to the family and friends of these prisoners...people who are equally angry and upset.

Their day will come. Perhaps not on this earth, but their day will come.

Until then, let's pray that they learn Paul's secret.

Grammy loved prisoners
Sunday, May 13, 2012

Early on Sunday morning, Mother's Day, as I think of my own mom, words to the old hymn OTHERS come to mind: **Lord, help me live from day to day in such a self-forgetful way, that even when I kneel to pray, my prayer shall be for others.**

Friends, relatives and family members of Mary Tjapkes were never forgotten, especially at times for birthdays or special need. There were hand-written notes, greeting cards and even baked goods. At the time of her funeral, we heard from people we had never met who at one time or another had been touched by my mother's kindness.

And so it was only natural that she had a love for prisoners. After all, Jesus demanded it.

She established a relationship with a prisoner by mail that lasted for some time. Naturally he was grateful for her kindness and generosity, and he reciprocated as best he could. Even back then, she told me of terrible conditions in the Michigan prison system, and the shameful manner in which prisoners were treated. But then came the major heart-break of getting emotionally involved with the least of these. One day, the letters stopped. After a period of time, Mom decided to get to the bottom of the story. She called the facility, only to be bluntly informed that the inmate had died. No details, no nothing. She said the man had no family, so she had no idea what happened after his death. She could find out nothing about his passing. She knew he had been frightened, so perhaps he lost his life in a violent manner. She never found out.

Maybe my mother's concern for and interest in prisoners started me on this journey. It certainly helped.

I pay tribute today to a very special mom, and grandmother, and great grandmother.

She touched many people.

Come to think of it, she still is.

Surrogate son

Saturday, May 12, 2012

I don't remember exactly when I began visiting Maurice Carter's mother for Mother's Day.

I began working on his case in about 1995, and it was a nine year battle to free him from prison. Over the years, as our relationship developed and we began calling each other "brother," it dawned on me that he couldn't visit his mom on Mother's Day. I promised him that I would visit her, in his place.

Elizabeth Fowler lived in a ramshackle dwelling in one of Gary, Indiana's, less pleasant neighborhoods. After my first visit it became apparent that she needed more than a visit. So in subsequent years, I would load up the car with groceries in addition to flowers and a greeting card. And even though it was up to me to purchase the flowers and the cards, I assured her that they came from Maurice, to which she always replied, "That Maurice, he's such a good boy."

As my retired pastor friend Al Hoksbergen became more friendly with Maurice and more versed about the case, I asked him to share this experience with me. We would go to see Mrs. Fowler not only on Mother's Day, but also at Christmas time. Each time we would bring flowers and gifts and greeting cards, but especially groceries. She was always pleased that I brought a pastor along, and loved to discuss spiritual matters.

When Maurice was alive and still in prison, he would call from the prison while we were there. What a delightful time that would be for his elderly mom, whose mind for the most part was able to stay relatively focused.

Al and I continued the practice after Maurice died in 2004, driving to Gary faithfully every Mother's Day and Christmas. We would not only stock up her kitchen, but we would remind her of the many wonderful memories of her son, talk about her faith, and say a prayer with her.

One day Mrs. Fowler was gone, and no one seems to know where. Maurice had a half-brother from another state who apparently decided his mother should come home with him. He came unannounced, told no one where he was taking her, and departed. We never saw her again, but because of her age we are assuming that she and Maurice are finally together again now.

But on Mother's Day, those memories will not fade. I used to tell Mrs. Fowler that if Maurice was my brother, she was then my adopted mother, and how she would laugh. And when I left her, the mandatory hug.

Precious memories.

No wonder he loved prisoners
Saturday, April 7, 2012

It's the night before Easter Sunday. I should be thinking about my Savior, and what he did for me. But I'm hurting. I'm reading a letter from a prisoner. He's terminally ill. He has cancer. We've been trying to help him obtain a commutation of his sentence. There's no reason for him to be there anymore. It would cost the state a fortune to treat him properly. He's certainly no threat to society. So what's the point?

The problem for Mr. C. is that he just can't get treatment. What the heck is wrong with us? Can't we give the guy the medicine he needs?

His simple letter just explains how sick he has become, and that recent tests at a Michigan hospital showed that his tumors are growing.

But then he complains about his chemo. First they gave him this. Then they gave him that. Than they decided to stop.

He enclosed copies of his many grievances, because it appears that all kinds of steps have been taken by the system to block his treatment. What's this all about? An oncologist ordered chemo, but a nurse got in the way and stopped it because there was a confusion over what day the treatment was to be received. So she wouldn't let him have it. And then it got to be five days after the treatment was ordered, he was in pain, and still no chemo.

I apologize on behalf of all free citizens. Our system is broken. God help us.

It's absolutely no wonder why Jesus felt such compassion for prisoners. This season reminds us that HE was wrongly convicted. In the process, he was terribly abused. And then wrongly executed.

We take our marching orders from the risen Lord.

He is risen! He is risen, indeed!

What Jesus didn't say
Sunday, March 11, 2012

I'm sitting here with my early Sunday morning cup of coffee, thinking about the words of Jesus specifically dealing with prisoners.

In Matthew 25, Jesus did not say, "I was a model prisoner, and you visited me."

He did not say, "I was of the same race, and so you visited me in prison."

He did not say, "I was a believer, a man of faith, and so you visited me."

Here at HFP, we take that to mean that our expression of love to prisoners must be unconditional.

This is on my mind this morning, because we're trying to help Ronnie. By his own mother's confession, he's been a bad apple. He gets in trouble. He gets tickets. The prison staff moved him to an unpleasant spot, where they keep trouble-makers. But there's something else. Ronnie may be dying. Because he's such a trouble-maker, he's not first in line to get appropriate treatment for his problems. But now his health issues are serious, and he's afraid of dying. Perhaps that's why he's now begging his mother to save him. He claims to be bleeding from every orifice, and even prison staffers admit to his mother that he's not in good shape.

And so we're trying to help. Regardless of his past behavior, his demeanor, his attitude, his track record, we claim that he deserves humane treatment and care.

We think that's what Jesus would have us do.

We're all in this together
Sunday, February 26, 2012

One of my favorite and oft-recited phrases took on new meaning yesterday.

Board Chair Dan Rooks, his wife Deb, and I, were special guests of Chapter 1014 of the National Lifers of America, in Michigan's huge women's facility. All 1,800 women incarcerated in Michigan are at Huron Valley in Ypsilanti. When community volunteer Mary Lynn Stevens invited me to speak at one of the chapter's monthly meetings, called a soiree, I readily accepted, and then asked if Dan and Deb could participate as well.

Saturday, the three of us were guests of honor at HVW, and it was one beautiful experience. We learned so much about their NLA chapter, and will talk more about it in the future. These women and this organization are amazing. To say that we were impressed would be an understatement.

But back to the title of this entry.

I do have manners, and the last thing I would ever do in a prison speech is hit on inmates for money. They don't have any. They are incredibly poor. Their expenses are high, and if I had it to send, I would send money to them.

But here's what happened. In my overview of HFP, I explained that we are facing a financial crunch. I told the women that in the past week I was forced to inform Dan that we had an uphill fight coming in March. We would have to raise $10,000 to stay in business, because we have used up our surplus. I honestly did this because, as I often say, we are all in this together, and I knew that many of these ladies would become prayer partners for our cause. I've had first-hand experience with this. Dozens of these women prayed for me during the staph infection health crisis of 2010.

One inmate tried to stop me right there in the speech, I got a little flustered but waited until Q&A time to respond. I hurried to the end of my presentation.

But the prisoner was not to be deterred. She wanted the address of HFP. Not sensing the connection, I put it up on the chalk board. Often prisoners ask for our address so that they may correspond with us.

Then another woman asked if she could send a contribution. Another asked if she could send a tithe. Still another asked if we were a tax-exempt agency. I started getting the picture and became alarmed. I quickly responded that I wasn't asking for that. Several more jumped into the fray and quickly said they understood, but they wanted to help. And then still another prisoner said, "We're talking about that $10,000 that you need."

I was dumbfounded. This wasn't heading in the right direction. I wanted to end my presentation, and then came the part that we may never get used to, the standing ovation. Cheering. Applause.

I'm going to tell you something. It's love.

True, we represented the love of Jesus with our presence there.

But there was love in the room. Not just respect. Not just kindness. There was love.

We were still feeling it all the way home.

One more reason why I love prisoners
Saturday, February 11, 2012

When I correspond with some of my friends in prison, I share personal information.

It's no secret that Marcia has been experiencing some health issues. They are not life-threatening, but they certainly do affect everyday living. And so, knowing that Marcia would be going to the University of Michigan Health Center for a certain procedure a week ago, I asked some of my Christian friends behind bars to pray for us.

Today Marcia received a letter from a Michigan prison.

Marcia:

I hope this letter finds you whole. About 18 of us came together a few days back and prayed for you. Your spirit, wisdom, and struggle has been a blessing to HFP, which has been a true blessing to us prisoners.

Be blessed,

Robert

Thank you, Robert, and thank you, prayer team of 18, for thinking of others, when your own situations aren't all that great.

God be near you.

Takes one to know one
Friday, December 9, 2011

I remember that as kids we threw that phrase back at someone who gave us a bad label. I'm reflecting on the phrase as I open the mail today, and I'm thinking there's some validity to it. I'm seeing incredible empathy for prisoners from those who are struggling with their own needs. Serious needs. Needs that might prevent you or me from functioning half-way normally. Needs that would definitely keep some people I know from even getting out of bed in the morning.

A beautiful supporter who is at an age where many would be sitting home in a rocker sipping tea instead placed an order for six prayer books to be placed into the hands of needy prisoners. She accompanied the order with a generous gift of support.

An African American supporter who has a son in prison and visits her best friend in prison got talking with another prison mom, and today they ordered five books for prisoners.

A supporter on total disability with more health problems than I could list in one article and no money, but with a blessed spirit that only Jesus could give, felt led to send us a check of support because she knows the pain of prisoners.

An elderly woman whose husband had to write the letter for her because she suffered a debilitating stroke, still felt the need to help others after reading of our ministry, and placed a check in the mail.

I am touched.

These aren't people caught up in the Christmas shopping frenzy. These are people who, despite their own set of problems, feel a kinship with men and women behind bars and want to demonstrate their love in a tangible way.

No one has to explain Matthew 25 to them. They get it.

Remembering Maurice Carter
Tuesday, October 25, 2011

I could envision a beautiful building perhaps in the style of the Supreme Court structure, with letters carved in marble or granite: THE MAURICE HENRY CARTER INSTITUTE FOR JUSTICE. Perhaps it would be located on the campus of my favorite college, Calvin in Grand Rapids. It would house Michigan's finest Innocence Project, handling cases with and without DNA evidence. Pre-law college students would fight on behalf of indigent prisoners claiming wrongful conviction. But the institute would go beyond that. It would help those who had fallen through the cracks, and had no family, no friends, to stand beside them in fighting for fair treatment, medical care, a halt to mental health abuse, etc., etc. It would fulfill every dream of Maurice Carter, who insisted that his negative had to be turned into a positive. It would be funded by foundations and trusts with never a financial worry. That's what I was dreaming exactly 7 years ago today.

I had already spent my final moments alone with Maurice in a Spectrum critical care unit. He was attached to every piece of equipment the hospital had that might be able to keep him alive for a few more minutes. But the staph infection was obviously winning. His frail, tired body finally gave up. Just past midnight, October 25, 2004.

I hadn't expected his death. I expected that he and I would work side by side to help prisoners. I did not expect to be carrying this torch alone. And so the organization, at that time named INNOCENT, continued its work. Later we changed the name to HUMANITY FOR PRISONERS to better reflect our mission. We incorporated as a Michigan non-profit agency. We obtained IRS approval for tax exemption. But the Carter dream didn't evolve into a major justice institute. Instead, we're a tiny agency with a huge heart, located in a single-room office, but carrying out the Carter dream with an amazing panel of professionals, a band of

196

committed volunteers, and a loyal albeit limited crowd of supporters who faithfully see that the bills get paid.

But as I reflect on Maurice's life and his dream on this meaningful day, I believe he would be pleased. I feel him at my side.

An African American gospel singer whom I loved and who died far too early in life, Alma Perry, used to sing this song. It doesn't exactly apply, but this is the spirit in which we carry on from day to day.

If I can help somebody as I pass along,
If I can cheer somebody, with a word or song,
If I can show somebody, how they're traveling
wrong,
Then my living shall not be in vain.

We're on the job, Maurice. Rest in peace.

On employing prisoners
Thursday, October 6, 2011

I would like to tell you about a genuine hero.

She certainly would not let us use her name, nor would she let us disclose the identity of her former employer.

We can tell you that she was employed in a supervisory position at a reputable company here in the western half of Michigan. Among the entry-level employees for whom she was responsible was a guy who voluntarily disclosed to her that he had served time in prison. She thanked him for the information but said it made no difference to her. He was a good employee, and did his job well without complaint. She stated her position, that he had served his time, and the past was the past. He thanked her, but said he just wanted her to know because all supervisors don't feel that way.

Well, sure enough, someone complained to the company that one of its employees was a former prisoner. And, the mid-level manager ordered the man's supervisor to fire him. She refused. Instead, she went to the top, explained the situation, said that the man had done nothing wrong and didn't deserve to be let go. Sadly, she didn't get support, even from the big boss. She was ordered to dismiss her employee. Again she refused, and instead resigned.

The man was still fired.

Two postscripts.

Number one, the top level manager who ordered the firing claimed to be a part-time fundamentalist pastor, but informed the supervisor that he, too, had to do some things that were against his principles. I guess his job was more important to him than principle.

And number two, as if to demonstrate that God approved of her decision to get out, our friend later was extremely successful in her next position of employment, in an occupation that took her to numerous foreign countries.

It's a sad state of affairs, but I must tell you that it is very difficult for former prisoners to find work, and once they find it, to keep their jobs here in Michigan. And it won't change unless we become as courageous as the hero of our story.

Michigan's Scarlet Letter
Saturday, September 3, 2011

One of the first prisoners ever to receive assistance from HUMANITY FOR PRISONERS, back in the days when the agency was still known as INNOCENT!, shamefully wears Michigan's Scarlet Letter. His name is on the sex offender registry.

Mr. J. sent me a curt message from his computer this week.

Yesterday, someone called my employer yet again...fourth time I lost a job in the last year because someone keeps calling my employers to tell them I am on the sex offender registry. Apparently the Scarlet Letter is alive and well.

Some steps have been taken to improve Michigan's poorly structured and poorly managed sex offender list. There are arguments for and against a state registry, but we have yet to see the perfect program.

There is no proof for this, but it seems like one could make a case that the state does everything it can to make it difficult for former prisoners to get a life in the real world upon their release. In fact, it seems to us that the state relishes the idea of getting prisoners to trip up. In a state where prison population is too high, and where budget is such a huge problem, you'd think that the state would do everything in its power to, one, adequately prepare prisoners who eventually will be released to make the re-entry successful; two, take all steps possible to make the re-entry smooth and barrier free; and three, prepare society in advance so that we know how to best help those freed prisoners in their difficult adjustment to a new life.

Continued steps to modify and improve Michigan's Scarlet Letter would be huge.

God bless those who are trying. There are too few of them, and their efforts are shamefully inadequate.

Thinking would help
Wednesday, August 3, 2011

I got a call this week from a guy who admits he broke the law. He's on the later side of middle-aged, and was growing some wacky tobacky in his back yard. I'm not sure why people think they can get away with this stuff, but that's another story. Anyway, he got arrested and convicted. But then he got sent to prison for a couple years. That, in itself, doesn't make a lot of sense. But now you gotta hear the rest.

The man had been injured several years earlier in a snowmobile accident, and is paralyzed from the waist down. This means that he cannot get around. It also means that he has problems with bowels and his urinary tract.

Now stop to think about it for a minute.

I know that this well-meaning judge wanted to get terrible criminals off the street. But guess how many problems it might cause not only for the new prisoner, but for the current occupants of the prison and for the prison staff, to suddenly admit this man. And when you get done thinking about that, stop to think about how much more this is going to cost the state than housing a healthy human being.

The results were completely predictable.

Prisoners couldn't stand having this guy around, with all of his personal hygiene issues, and they finally took things into their own hands and beat the guy to a pulp. That was their only solution to the problem. The man recites a litany of disasters that no one should have had to experience. His punishment turned out to be much worse than the actual crime.

There has to be a better way. This is sheer stupidity.

202

In a case like this, it's hard to believe that anyone was thinking.

I'll say a prayer for you
Friday, July 1, 2011

How often do you make that statement, when someone shares a need or a problem with you? It's often how Christians respond. It's kind and reassuring. It's what we do for each other. And then we go about praying for this person or this need in private.

I must tell you about an experience yesterday.

I was speaking with a Christian brother in prison, and we were talking about the status of my health. This has been a topic of concern for the past year, after a one-year battle with a staph infection. I nearly lost my life several times.

I'm grateful now for every day of my new life. BUT, as I shared with my friend in prison, I get very nervous now when a minor health issue comes up. For example, I have been troubled with, what I believe, was just a bout with the flu this week. But I immediately worry that the staph infection may be returning. As I explained that to Mike, he interrupted me and immediately launched into a brief prayer for me! He didn't say "I'll be praying for you." He did it. And I was touched as I sat listening to him claim the promises of Jesus, praying for good health and calmness of spirit for me.

It's not really that hard to do, this business of living our Christianity right up front...we're just not used to doing it.

That's the way my friend in prison lives. His Christianity is more exemplary than mine.

I share the story because I see it time and again. There are beautiful Christians behind bars. May we never forget it.